ESSAYS ON ZARATHUSTRA
AND ZOROASTRIANISM

Bibliotheca Iranica

Zoroastrian Studies Series, No. 1

Prods Oktor Skjærvø, General Editor

JEAN KELLENS

ESSAYS ON
ZARATHUSTRA
AND
ZOROASTRIANISM

Translated and Edited By
Prods Oktor Skjærvø

MAZDA PUBLISHERS, Inc.
2000

Mazda Publishers, Inc.
Academic publishers since 1980
P.O. Box 2603
Costa Mesa, California 92626 U.S.A.
www.mazdapublishers.com

Library of Congress Cataloging-in-Publication Data

Kellens, Jean.

Essays on Zarathustra and Zoroastrianism/ Jean Kellens; translated and edited by Prods
Oktor Skjærvø.

p.cm—(Bibliotheca Iranica: Zoroastrian Studies Series, No. 1)

Includes bibliographical references.

ISBN: 1-56859-129-2

(softcover: alk. paper)

1. Zoroastrianism. I. Skjærvø, Prods O. II. Title. III. Series.

BL1571.K445 2000

295—dc21

00-042731

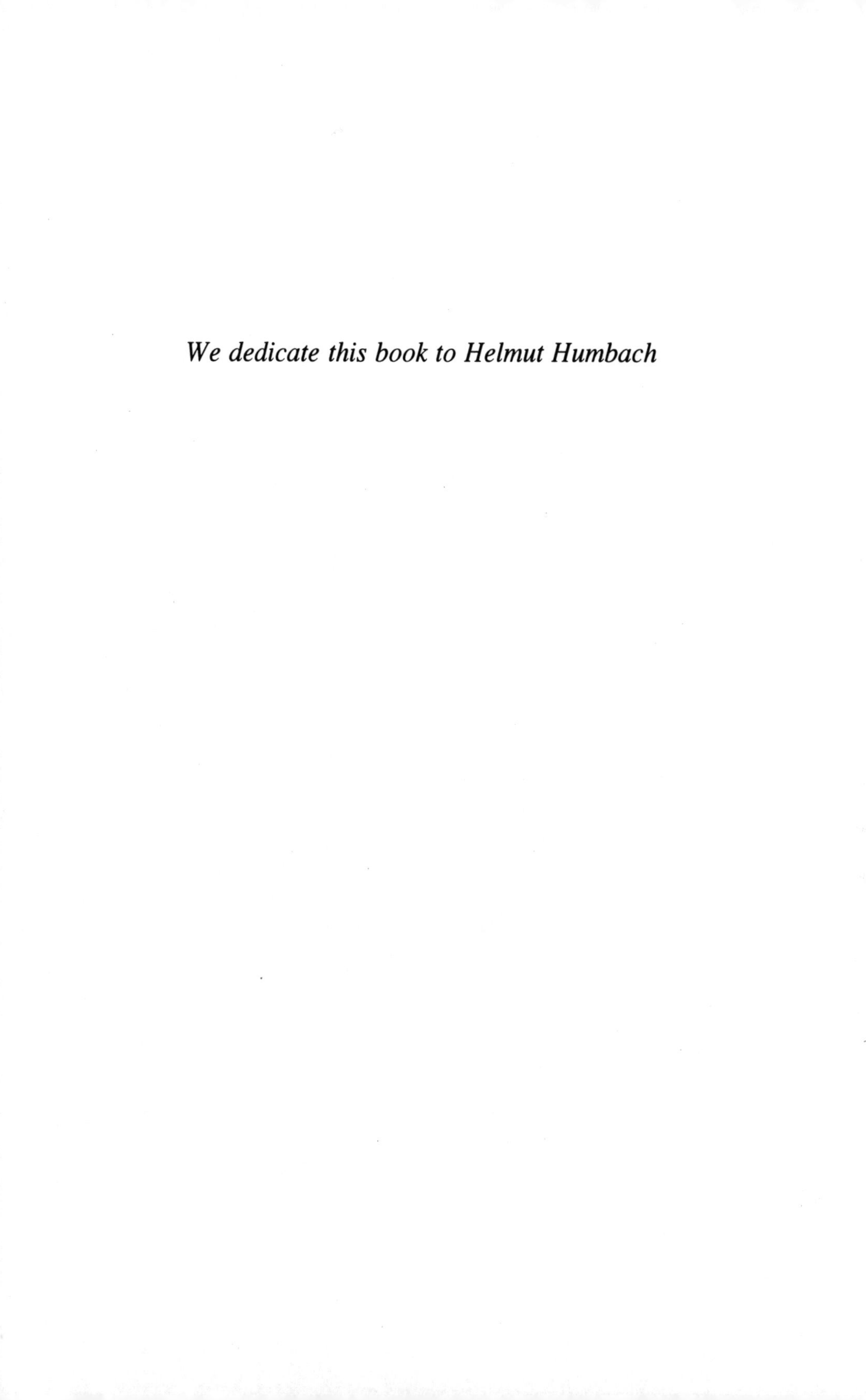

CONTENTS

ACKNOWLEDGMENTS

"Characters of Ancient Mazdaism," first published in *History and Anthropology* 3, 1987, pp. 239-262, © Harwood Academic Publishers GmBH, 1987, is reprinted with the permission of Gordon and Breach Publishers.

"Achaemenid Religion: Preliminary Questions," was translated from "Questions préalables," in J. Kellens, ed., *La religion iranienne à l'époque achéménide. Actes du Colloque de Liège 11 décembre 1987*, Iranica Antiqua, Suppl. 5, Gent, 1991, pp. 81-86, © 1990 by Iranica Antiqua, and is published with the permission of Peeters Publishers and Booksellers, Leuven.

Zarathustra and the Old Avesta. Four Lectures at the Collège de France, was translated from *Zoroastre et l'Avesta ancien. Quatre leçons au Collège de France*, Travaux de l'Institut d'Études Iraniennes de l'Université de la Sorbonne Nouvelle 14, Paris, 1991, and is published with the permission of the l'Institut d'Études Iraniennes de l'Université de la Sorbonne Nouvelle.

"Yima and Death," was translated from "Yima et la mort," in M. A. Jazayery and W. Winter, eds., *Languages and Cultures. Studies in Honor of Edgar C. Polomé*, Berlin, New York, Amsterdam: Mouton de Gruyter, 1988, pp. 329-34, and is published with the permission of Mouton de Gruyter, A Division of Walter de Gruyter GmBH & Co. KG Publishers.

"The Speculative Ritual in Ancient Mazdaism," was translated from "Le rituel spéculatif du mazdéisme ancien," in J. Kellens and C. Herrenschmidt, "La question du rituel dans le mazdéisme ancien et achéménide," *Archives de Sciences sociales des Religions* 85, 1994, pp. 45-67, and is published with the permission of the Archives de Sciences sociales des Religions, Centre de la Recherche Scientifique – Écoles des Hautes Études en Sciences Sociales, Paris.

The typescript was composed with Microsoft Word 5.1 for the Macintosh and Euroiranica font, © Ecological Linguistics, and printed on a Hewlett Packard Laserjet 2100 M.

Editor's Foreword

I began translating Kellens's work in order to make it accessible to my students in Old Iranian Religion, many of whom, at the time they attend the classes, do not know French well enough to be able to read complicated technical literature. I soon conceived the idea of making a translation for publication of the entire *Zoroastre et l'Avesta ancien* (1991), as being a more mature analysis and synthesis of the Old Iranian texts and religion than those presented in J. Kellens and E. Pirart's pioneering edition of *Les textes vieil-avestiques* (1988-1991), some of the conclusions of which, though tentative, were being widely cited to discredit the entire edition. While engaged in this work, it also became clear, however, that this book alone was insufficient for my purposes: on one hand, it did not cover all those of Kellens's contributions to the field that I wanted the students to read, some of which were referenced in the book, and, on the other hand, some of the ideas were already being overtaken by Kellens's more recent research. I therefore added the articles translated here, as well as one originally written in English.

There is obviously some repetition, as in the case of the passages devoted to the explanation of *cinuuatō pǝrǝtu-*, but in each such instance the perspective or context is different, or the author's thoughts have developed. I have therefore not found it necessary to substitute internal references for the repeated passages.

The editing task has been confined to standardizing the transcriptions* and references throughout, including "Characters of Ancient Mazdaism," and compiling a bibliography. I have also lightly edited "Characters" to bring its style and format into line with the rest of the book (standard American English spelling and punctuation). The decision to include a complete bibliography of Kellens's publications followed naturally.

For the convenience of the reader I have added a few footnotes containing information not given in the text. These and a few other remarks by the editor are enclosed in square brackets. In "The speculative ritual" I have

---

* Note: *maniiu-*, etc., instead of *mainiiu-* or *mañiiu-* is just a simplifying convention.

added sub-headings for greater clarity.   All these additions have been approved by Kellens.

I am pleased to offer this book as the first in this new Zoroastrian Studies Series, thus making available to students, as well as the general public—not least the Iranian and Zoroastrian communities themselves—what I think is the most important *novel* work on the Old Avesta and the Old Iranian religion to have appeared during the last quarter century and to have paved the way to a more balanced discussion of the entire issue in the new millennium.

Prods Oktor Skjærvø
Cambridge, Massachusetts
4 November 1999.

Author's Preface

(1999)

The articles gathered in this volume, centered around the four lectures I gave at Collège de France in late 1989, represent the various attempts I made between 1987 and 1994 to provide a synthesis of Mazdaism, the Old Iranian religion. The thoughts I developed in these articles were inspired by a joint project with Eric Pirart begun in 1982 and concluded in 1991, namely a systematic analysis of the Old Avestan texts. As the opinions expressed there naturally varied as this analysis evolved, I have to make a few things clear, even at the presumptuous risk of writing my own history.

"Characters of Ancient Mazdaism" was my contribution to a CNRS* project that aimed at showing that polytheism is "unthinkable" for a modern scholar. It is the first time I evinced my skepticism toward the reality, or at least the importance, of the "Zoroastrian reform," although today I regard that article as having only an anecdotal interest. Under the influence of Helmut Humbach's *Die Gathas des Zarathustra* (1959) I underestimated to the point of denial the eschatological part of Avestan Mazdaism (as I still did in the chapter on *The Text* in the introduction to Kellens-Pirart, 1988, pp. 3-41). The extreme importance of the eschatology soon became clear, however, and I explained my ideas in "L'eschatologie mazdéenne ancienne" (1994), my contribution to the Irano-Judaica colloquium in Jerusalem in July 1990. The conclusions in this article were incorporated in *Zoroastre et l'Avesta ancien* (1991, pp. 48-51) and "Le rituel spéculatif du mazdéisme ancien" (1994, p. 49).** Anyway, today I find the discussion about whether

---

* [The French Centre National de la Recherche Scientifique.]

** These two texts also incorporate the hypothesis that *maniiu-* means "opinion" ("Un avis sur vieil-avestique *mainiiu-*," 1990; pp. 116-117 of this article are translated below in n. 70), that is, opinion about the nature of the cosmos, for which Skjærvø in his lectures on Old Iranian literature at the École Pratique des Hautes Études, Sorbonne, Paris, May 1997, proposed "inspiration." [Currently I think the *maniiu* reflects both meanings of *inspiration*: the process and its effect/result; the latter would in practice be the *inspired opinion* about the

xiii

Mazdaism is polytheistic, monotheistic, or dualistic both simplistic and not critical enough, and I find these grand, but summary, classifications meaningless in the scholarly discourse and, at any rate, completely inadequate for explaining the Mazdean pantheon.

"Questions préalables" was a talk given at the colloquium on Iranian religion in the Achaemenid period which was held at Liège, December 11, 1987. There is nothing in it that I would like to change now, other than, perhaps, the perspective of some details. I also recognize that my tone may have been a bit provocative (as pointed out by Gnoli in his review, 1992, pp. 528-529), but this was due to my frustration at having for so long grappled with the problem of whether the Achaemenids were Zoroastrian or not, a problem I now consider purely academic and misleading. The recent article "Les achéménides dans le contexte indo-iranien" (1997) can be regarded as an updated, and more composed, version of that article.

The first two of my four lectures at Collège de France are, of all the texts gathered here (except the last), the ones with which I have remained most in agreement. The first (The Text) contains my vision of the history of Old Avestan studies and the second (The Gods) my interpretation of the system of the Aməṣa Spəntas, to which the *yasna*, that is, the litany in *yazamaidē*, of the *Yasna Haptaŋhāiti*, bears witness in a precise and decisive fashion. This lecture did not, however, contain a global analysis of the Mazdean pantheon. I have since completed the analysis in my book on the Old Avestan pantheon (*Le panthéon de l'Avesta ancien*, 1994), which had been prepared to some extent by my article on Old Avestan *hātąm* ("Le sens de vieil-avestique *hātąm*," 1989). In this article I recognized in certain expressions based upon the stylization of the verb "to be" a way of referring to the gods without mentioning their names, in the framework of a ritual system of rules which, without hostility, did not allow the secondary gods to be mentioned in the sacrifice to the dominant god.

The third lecture (The Liturgy) may be regarded as my conception of Mazdean dualism, which means that Shaul Shaked's (1994, p. 8 n. 6) criticisms aimed at me on this issue have now lost their target. Without

---

cosmos, which was basically Kellens's position! (Skjærvø)] Since then I have been quite preoccupied with the eschatology of the Young Avesta, both the individual eschatology ("L'âme entre le cadavre et le paradis," 1995) and the collective eschatology ("De la naissance des montagnes à la fin du temps: le Yašt 19," 1989).

entering upon a new discussion of this central question (see now "La strophe des jumeaux," 1997, pp. 65-67), I confess that today our reading of this text leaves me with mixed feelings. The motif of the cosmic hut, which I think I glimpse in the Old Avestan texts (since "Huttes cosmiques en Iran," 1989), is based upon two strange words found only in obscure contexts, as justly pointed out by Mary Boyce (1992, p. 61 n. 16). Nevertheless, I believe it is there because of some more certain terms, though more rare and never associated in a manner to form a cohesive image (for instance, *viiā-* and *dəbązah-*). We seem to find ourselves in a situation where the text makes suggestions, but lacks the precise information we need to formulate a firm hypothesis.

In "Yima et la mort" I interpreted the expression *cinuuatō pərətu-* as "the bridge of him who makes a heap/pile," the "one who makes a heap/pile" being the one who piled up stones to make a ford. I am still convinced that this is the only legitimate grammatical analysis, for I do not think that the fact that Persian *cīn-/cīdan* means primarily "gather, collect" necessarily implies that Avestan *cinao-/cinu-* could mean "choose, select, make a choice." I very much doubt that the Old Iranian farmers harvested the way Jean-Jacques picked cherries at Madam de Warens's and defined their activities by *selection* rather than *making a heap*. I still wonder about the identity of this builder, however, since it is difficult to see how this motif fits into the Avestan myth of Yima.

"Le rituel spéculatif du mazdéisme ancien" is by far the most recent of these articles. Having had no time to distance myself from it sufficiently to view it critically, I consider it as a kind of state of the art. Many have taken exception to my ritualistic interpretation of the *Gāθās*, which has not bothered me (see "La strophe des jumeaux," 1997, pp. 64-65 with n. 62). The few rearrangements I have made in favor of dualism and eschatology have not brought me to a reevaluation of the texts with less emphasis on the ritual aspect. Not only are all Mazdean concepts known to us through liturgical texts, but they are articulated together with the performance of the ritual, which constantly stresses the dualist opposition or entails the eschatology. That is why I stress the fact that the old Mazdean ritual is speculative.

It remains to comment upon my position with regard to Zarathustra's historicity. I admitted it in "Characters of Ancient Mazdaism," while rejecting his role as singer and author, and still did so in the introduction to *Les textes vieil-avestiques* (vol. 1, 1988, pp. 3-41). I was much more suspicious of it in "Questions préalables" and in the chapter on "Les hommes" in *Zoroastre et l'Avesta ancien* (1991). My hesitation was due to the fact that I was not yet entirely freed from the argument put forth since Martin Haug for making Zarathustra into an historical prophet, namely the impression that he appears as a human and contemporary personality in the *Gāθās*, but in the later tradition as a fantastic hero. This would imply, of course, that the *Gāθās* describe a contemporary reality, while the Young Avesta and the Pahlavi books tell a history that had deteriorated into legend. Today I believe that there is in this matter neither history nor legend, but that our documentary strata all equally report the elements of a myth. To see this it suffices to defend oneself against the impression of reality that comes from the 20th-century translations of the *Gāθās* and instead look at the strange rhetorical similarities they present with the Young Avesta. Each *Gāθā* shares with the *yašts*, such as *Yašt* 5, a catalog of sacrificers. The question is of course to know why, when reproducing this traditional scheme, they limit it to the companions of Zarathustra. The task in coming years of those who are not irrationally obsessed by the personality of Zarathustra is, therefore, to study the literary practices in the Old Avesta and to try to analyze the myth of Zarathustra. The first attempts in this sense have just appeared: see P. O. Skjærvø's "Zarathustra in the Avesta and in Manicheism" (1996) and "The Literature of the Most Ancient Iranians" 1996 [publ. 1997], as well as my "De la naissance des montagnes" (1989).

I am happy to conclude on this note, expressing the affinities that link me with the translator of these texts. I am honored and pleasantly confused that Prods Oktor Skjærvø has deemed it useful to spend his time on this work, and I lack words to express my admiration for the result.

Jean Kellens
Collège de France
19 February 1999

Characters of Ancient Mazdaism
(1987)

WHEN, UNDER MOSLEM PRESSURE, Mazdaism collapsed in the land of its origin, the canon of sacred texts had been assembled for only a short time. The Sasanian clergy, completing a task that had been started perhaps under the Arsacid dynasty,[1] had collected the hitherto oral texts, arranged them according to liturgical use, invented an *ad hoc* alphabet, and put into writing a unique and *ne varietur* version of the book they had thus constituted.[2] The book was given the name *abestāg*, which the Parsis later turned into *avesta* and which probably comes from the Old Iranian **upastāvaka* "praise (of Ahura Mazdā)."[3] In the eighteenth century, Anquetil-Duperron went to India, found the corrupted legacy and offered it up to the reflections of Western scholarship.

The *Avesta* is not a homogeneous book. It is an assorted mixture, whose layers are so numerous and intertwined that it is difficult, if not impossible, to discern its structure and trace its history. It is at least quite clear that one of the three major parts of the book, the *Yasna* or "offering," contains a short corpus of texts, in metric verse (*Gāθā*) and prose (*Yasna Haptaŋhāiti*), which differ from the rest both in the concepts that are expressed and in the language. The language presents archaic traits that induce us, looking at the degree of evolution of other Old Iranian dialects, to define it as "Old Avestan" and to situate it between 800 and 1200 B.C., the two extremes being the least likely.

---

1   [Ca. 247 B.C.E. - 224 C.E.]

2   Most recently on this subject see Sundermann, 1985, p. 112. It is generally admitted, after Bailey (1943, pp. 191-193), that the invention of the Avestan alphabet took place in the late Sasanian period, in the 5th or 6th century. According to paleographic evidence, it could have been as early as 430 (Hoffmann, 1975, p. 317).

3   This is Bartholomae's hypothesis (1905, p. 108).

The *Gāθās*, the oldest evidence of the language and religion of ancient Iran, have become a very popular text.[4] Since the turn of the century, when Avestan was endowed with its major works of reference,[5] the *Gāθās* have undergone seven attempts at interpretation, to count only the serious ones.[6] The latest, published in 1975 by Stanley Insler, received so much criticism and praise at the same time that it is evident that Western scholarship is far from reaching a consensus, even an approximate one, on the content of their message. The difficulty of this text lies in its brevity and its isolation. It is not long: seventeen hymns made up of fifteen stanzas, which is obviously too little to elucidate entirely the processes of a learned and sophisticated rhetoric. It stands alone: the *Avesta* is a monument situated outside time and space upon which no historical or archeological document can be brought to bear. Dating its constituent parts can be attempted only by approximation, on the basis of linguistic arguments alone. The Old Avestan part is even more ethereal. Not only are there no allusions to historical events or geographical places, not even mythical ones, but, for the language as for the religious concepts, there is a complete break between this part and the Young Avesta, more recent by several centuries, about which nothing at all is known. Under such conditions, what is an appropriate method for deciphering the language of this text and defining its religious content? From the point of view of linguistic analysis, comparison with the Vedic hymns of India is doubtlessly advisable: this is the approach that has produced all of the important steps that have been made, from Bartholomae to Insler. It is, on the other hand, useless for analyzing content, since the *Gāθās* apparently are the expression of a radical change in religious ideas that looks like a revolution with respect to the Indo-Iranian religion, whose most faithful image is considered to be the Rigveda. Western scholarship

---

4   The prose of *Yasna Haptaŋhāiti* is not written in a language that differs fundamentally from the *Gāθās*, but its religious conceptions seem more advanced and designate it as being slightly more recent. On the other hand, this text has been largely neglected, the only general study devoted to it being Baunack's (1888).

5   Critical edition: K. F. Geldner, *Avesta, the Sacred Book of the Parsis*, 3 vols., Stuttgart, 1889-96; grammar: C. Bartholomae, in *Grundriss der Iranischen Philologie*, Strassburg, 1896; dictionary: C. Bartholomae, *Altiranisches Wörterbuch*, Strassburg, 1904.

6   Bartholomae, 1905; Andreas-Wackernagel, 1909-31; Maria Wilkins Smith, 1929; Duchesne-Guillemin, 1948; Humbach, 1959; Lommel, 1971; Insler, 1975.

decided to seek enlightenment from the historical Mazdean tradition, which recognizes the *Gāθās* as its founding text. Without exception, all of the analysts—Humbach somewhat more prudently—chose to measure the text by the yardstick of tradition. Such a choice is neither legitimate nor illegitimate: it is a mere wager. We do not know if the tradition is reliable and if, once rid of the distortions inevitable when ideas evolve and freed of the legendary outcroppings that come to decorate the original account, it gives a faithful description of its early history; or if, in its obscure progress down through the centuries (fourteen!), it underwent ruptures that rendered it more ignorant and defenseless than even we ourselves.

The *Gāθās* have thus often been explained deductively, the method being to see if the imperfectly understood passages either might not illustrate an episode of the life of Zarathustra as related by the Sasanian church, or might not express an idea he is considered by tradition to have invented. Three main postulates are emitted concerning the meaning of the Old Avestan texts:

1. The *Gāθās* are the work of one person. Their author, Zarathustra, conceived by historical analogy as a prophet (Judaism) or a reformer (Protestantism), condemns the religion of his times, preaching to a royal family a new, highly moral and spiritual doctrine. The conversion of the royalty ensures the support of temporal power and opens the way for success.

2. The Old Avestan religious system is distinguished from the old Indo-Iranian religion, as well as from later Mazdaism, by its affirmation of a kind of monotheism with a more or less clear tendency towards dualism.

3. Zarathustra lends particular importance to individual and collective eschatology: human life ends with its reward in heaven or its punishment in hell; the world will undergo a last judgment which consecrates the destruction of evil and the final victory of good.[7]

---

[7] Dualism and eschatology thus conceived assume the existence of the abstract ideas of good and evil. It is known that Zarathustra generally is thought to have been the first to have set up this opposition and that is why Nietzsche, admittedly and ironically enough, used him as a mouthpiece. In fact, the *Gāθās* provide no sure attestation of the opposition between good and evil. Here again everything depends on the solution proposed to a problem of phraseology: does the absolute use of the adjective *vohu-* "good," or its degrees *vahiiah-* and *vahišta-*, refer to the abstract idea of good or, by ellipsis, to a word that is understood and usually

All of this is obviously familiar. A German colleague once voiced his surprise that the *Gāθās* seem infinitely closer to us than the Vedic texts, whereas they both make use of similar formulaic material and rhetorical techniques. This paradox should be a warning. One is obliged to wonder if the religious universe of the *Gāθās* doesn't seem familiar only because we are the ones who have peopled it. In what follows, I propose to examine this question with respect to the second and third postulates—the first, and not the least questionable, concerns the historical dimension of the *Gāθās* and is not the subject of our discussion. Only one approach is suitable for this process of verification: an attempt should be made, not to shed light on the *Gāθās* from the outside, but to make the best of the meaning offered by the text as we understand it. This is not an impracticable method, as Humbach applied it to a certain extent and with happy results. It is sometimes powerless, because it happens, at times, that the Old Avestan resists analysis, but it is not any more ineffective than the deductive method; moreover, our method enables us to take a different approach to the many obscure passages which are difficult in part because the meaning postulated does not coincide with the linguistic information.

Using the eschatological assumption, the commentators of the *Gāθās* recognize in many of the abstract words terms relating to life after death or to the final destiny of humanity.[8] At least three words may mean "recompense" (reward): *aši-*, *ādā-*, and *mīžda-*; three others, "salut" (salvation) or "œuvre finale" (final work): *sauua(h)-*, *yāh-*, and *maga-*. This abundance of synonyms in a language of limited lexicon is most troubling, and it is of no reassurance to see that the meaning attributed to these words rarely

---

characterized by the adjective? I can not examine the question here and will simply say that the second solution is sometimes obvious and always plausible.

8 Another effect of this postulate is the abnormally high number of verbal categories reputed able to express the future. These include not only the present and aorist subjunctives, which, although they do indeed express the unaccomplished aspect, have no exact translation in the French or German use of the simple future, but also present and aorist injunctives, that, as is now known, have nothing to do with the future (Hoffmann, 1967; Humbach used the conclusions of this study prior to its publication). In fact, the Old Avestan verbal system was never subjected to a precise analysis, and the eschatological postulate stands in for rigorous doctrine. In a revealing manner, translators render the forms of the injunctive by the future or the preterite according to the meaning they attribute to the context ...

corresponds to what etymology seems to indicate. Of course, it is not legitimate to expect that an Old Avestan word would always have the same meaning as its Vedic equivalent: there may be semantic divergences of a dialectal kind between the Indian and the Iranian words, an evolution or specification of meaning in one language or the other. Nevertheless, the etymology alone provides a clue when the contexts are not sufficiently clear or meaningful to reveal the sense of a word, and this clue, according to each case, makes it possible to carry the analysis further, to develop a hypothesis, or better than not doing anything, settle on an approximation. It is indisputably to Humbach's credit that he foremost and always takes his cue from etymology, which has led him to restrict considerably the role eschatology plays in Gathic doctrine. Of all the above-cited words, only *mīžda-*, equivalent of the Vedic *mīḍhá-* and the Greek *misthós*, incontestably means "recompense" (reward).[9] In three passages, *mīžda-* is used as a direct object of the verb *han*, "to acquire," in a significant expression, "deserve a salary." The nature of this salary is specified twice. These are tangible goods:

Y.44.18
dasā aspå aršənuuaitīš uštrəmcā
   "ten mares with a stallion and a camel";

Y.46.19
gāuuā azī
   "two cows with calf,"

but they may have had a symbolic value since, in Y.44.18 they are associated, perhaps metaphorically identified,[10] with physical integrity and immortality (*hauruuātā amərətātā*) in a concept that persists in the Young Avesta:

Yt.1.25
hauruuata amərətāta yōi stō mīždəm ašaonąm
   "the integrity and immortality that are the reward of the followers of Aša."

---

9   See also the later Persian *muzd* "salary."

10 The unclear meaning of one word (*apiuuaitī*) in the context makes it impossible to decide with certainty.

It can be concluded from Y.34.13 that *mīžda* is one of the gifts that are attainable by following the way opened by the ritual between the gods and men:

> *təm aduuānəm ahurā yəm mōi mraoš vaŋhəuš manaŋhō*
> *daēnå saošiiaṇtąm yā hū.kərətā aṣācīṭ uruuāxšaṭ*
> *hiiaṭ ciuuištā hudåbiiō mīždəm mazdā ...*
>> "this well-made path by which the consciences of those vowed to opulence make their way by Aṣa towards the reward you reserve for the bounteous, O Mazdā."

And again Y.49.9, in which religious consciences seek to acquire *mīžda* through ritual practices metaphorically expressed by the verb *yuj* "harness":

> *hiiaṭ daēnå vahištē yūjən mīždē / aṣā.yuxtā yāhī dəjāmāspā*
>> "when the sons of Djāmāspa harness their consciences for the very good reward."

mīžda is not only a benefit reserved for mankind, since Y.51.15 says that Zarathustra reserves it preferably for Ahura Mazdā:

> *hiiaṭ mīždəm zaraθuštrō magauuabiiō cōišt parā / garō dəmānē ahurō mazdå*
> *jasaṭ pouruiiō*
>> "Ahura Mazdā is the first to enter the dwelling of welcome, (coming) towards the reward that Zarathustra has refused to the *magauuan*."

In no Gathic passage does *mīžda* designate the fate that befalls the soul after death.[11] It is a reward that men and the gods accord each other mutually, during a sacrificial ceremony, in acknowledgment of a boon.

---

11 The only indication to the contrary would be the form *parāhūm* (Y.46.19) that is interpreted as the accusative of the adjective *parāhu-*, qualifying *mīžda-* and meaning "having to do with the future life," composed of *parā-* "before" and *ahu-* "existence." But this is only one evasive conjecture among others. Even if it were exact, the only conclusion that could be drawn would be that *mīžda-* can designate the *post mortem* reward if it is stated. One use of this kind is attested in the young Avesta, V.8.81: *cuuaṭ ahmāi naire mīždəm aŋhaṭ pasca astasca baoδaŋhasca vīuruuištīm* "what will be the value of the reward for a man after the separation of the body and the conscience?"

aṣi- occurs more frequently and has a considerably more brilliant future than *mīžda*, which subsists in Young Avestan only in rare passages inspired by the Gathic text. It designates an abstraction which sporadically accedes to the rank of entity (Y.31.4, perhaps Y.43.12 and Y.51.10) and in Young Avestan it is the name of a goddess of plenty, a deity of the third function, who receives a full *Yašt* (Yt.17). Bartholomae (1906, col. 241) paraphrases *aṣi-* rather than giving a translation: "was einem aufgrund seiner Leistung— in gutem und schlimmem Sinn zukommt; Anteil, Los, Verdienst, Lohn, Belohnung, bes. beim letzten Gericht."[12]   The etymological pattern of YAv. passages,

Y.9.3 (etc.)
kā ahmāi aṣiš ərənāuui
  "what share was shared out to him?"

and

Y.56.3
aṣōiš ... yā nə̄ āraēcā ərənauuataēcā
  "the share that was and will be shared out to us"

shows an abstract derivative in *-ti-* (*ṛti-*) from the root *ar* "to share out" (= Ved. *ṛnóti*). *aṣi* then designates something given out. It can be positive or negative:

Y.43.4
aṣīš drəguuāitē aṣāunaēcā
  "the share for the unfaithful and for the followers of Aṣa."

The content may be abstract or concrete:

Y.28.7
tąm aṣīm vaŋhə̄uš āiiaptā mananhō
  "this share: the favors of good thinking";

---

12 Smith: "reward," Duchesne-Guillemin: "rétribution," Lommel: "Belohnung"; Insler: "reward."

Y.43.1
rāiiō aṣīš
   "shares of wealth."

In the light of its etymology,[13] confirmed by the Young Avestan use exclusively in the context of the third function, *aṣi-* does not necessarily designate something given in retribution. It would seem that this is the case only once, in Y.43.5 where it is used as a synonym of *mīžda-*:

hiiaṯ då šiiaoθanā mīždauuąn yācā uxδā / akəm akāi vaŋ᷎hīm aṣīm vaŋhauuē
   "the fact that you have subjected the ritual acts to reward, (attributing) the
   bad (reward) to the bad (act) and the good share to the good (act)."

The most exact meaning is "octroi" (grant, share), as Humbach and Dumézil understood, Humbach systematically using the translation "Anteil" and Dumézil making it the equivalent of the Vedic *bhága-*, "part" (share, portion) (1977, pp. 120, pp. 145-146). The abstraction designated by *aṣi-* is not an eschatological reference. Its personification is associated with two entities who embody the good ritual behavior of man, Ārmaiti, "la juste prise en considération" (right estimation) and Sraoša "observance" (observance, keeping of a rule).

For *ādā-*, Bartholomae (cols. 320-321) proposes the sense "Vergeltung, Heimzahlung," specifying "insbes. beim Schlussgericht."[14] This word is attested four times in the old part of the Avesta but has left no descendants in the Iranian dialects—it appears twice in Young Avestan (Y.52.3, Y.68.21 = Vr.4.1), in conjunction with *aṣi-*, but these passages are inspired by the Old Avestan corpus. It is never mentioned in a meaningful context so that the sense of the word can only be approached through the etymology. *ādā-* has no Vedic equivalent, but it is clearly a noun of action, derived without suffix from the root *dā* "to place" and composed with the verbal prefix *ā*. Humbach's translation "Gabe," and Kellens's "oblation" (1974, pp. 208-210, after Narten's "Darbringung") are both imprecise in that they leave aside the prefix. *ā́-dā* is used in Old Avestan (Kellens 1984, pp. 26-27): in

---

13 *aṣi-* in the plural and modified by a genitive has the strictly etymological
   meaning of "mise en mouvement, envoi" (setting into motion, sending): thus
   Y.28.4 *aṣīšcā šiiaoθənanąm* "the sending of ritual acts" (see also Y.34.12).
14 Smith: "accounting," Duchesne-Guillemin: "rétribution," Lommel: "Vergeltung," Insler: "requital."

the active voice it means "to put in" (Ved. *á-dhā)*, in the middle voice, "to receive" (Ved. *ā-dā*). Since a derivative of the latter would be a pleonasm in Y.33.12

> *dasuuā ... mazdā vaŋhuiiā zauuō ādā*
> "receive, O Mazdā, vivacity, by way of good *ādā*,"

a meaning of *ādā* coherent with that of the verb *ā-dā* in Y.34.3 must be postulated:

> *at̰ tōi miiazdəm ahurā nəmaŋhā aṣ̌āicā dāmā / gaēθå vispå ā xšaθrōi*
> "for thee, O Ahura, and for Aṣ̌a, we lay down, as a solid offering, all the flocks in thy control"

and one fitting the locative use in Y.33.11:

> *mərəždātā mōi ādāi kahiiācḭ̄t paitī*
> "have mercy on me at each *ādā*"[15]

It is quite likely that *ādā-* designates a moment in a ritual when the offering is laid down.

On the words *sauua-* and *sauuah-*, which are perhaps only two stems of a heteroclite, etymology provides contradictory clues. They are clearly derived from the root *sū*, the equivalent of the Vedic *śū: śváyati* "to inflate," but the Pahlavi translator renders them by the related term *swt* "profit, utility, advantage."[16]

The question is, then, whether the Avestan verb is intransitive like its Indian equivalent, or transitive like its Middle Iranian descendent. In other words, is the divergence a chronological one, with the old Indo-Iranian

---

[15] The sense "reward at the last judgment" is in open contradiction with the indefinite adjective *kahiiācḭ̄t*, which marks *ādāi (ka- + cḭt)* "all ... whatever it may be."

[16] The verb itself is only attested once in Old Avestan (Y.51.9). The question occupying us is, alas, an ambiguous one, since it concerns a form derived from the present stem *sauuaiia-*, which can be considered as a primary stem or a causative. *saošiiaṇt-* is an important derivative traditionally held to be a term that, from the *Gāθās* on, designates the future saviors who will bring about the renewal of the world. I challenged this interpretation twelve years ago (1974, pp. 187-209) and, to a certain extent, it is that analysis that I have summarized here.

dialects having an intransitive verb, or a dialectal one in which the Iranian verb differs from the Indian verb in being transitive. At the end of the nineteenth century, those of the Vedic school naturally opted for the first solution: Bartholomae (1882, p. 108) and Geldner (1884, p. 70) translated *sū* by "gedeihen." In 1904, in the *Altiranisches Wörterbuch* (cols. 1561-62), Bartholomae changed his mind and translates *sauua(h)-* by "Nutzen, Vorteil," qualified by "der ewige im andern Leben"; this was to become the authorized meaning.[17]

Humbach alone sticks with the intransitive ("Kraft"), according to Hoffmann (1952, p. 15, n. 15). Two Young Avestan derivatives of *sū* provide an irreproachable argument in favor of the intransitive hypothesis. No one has ever claimed that the adjective *sūra-*, which defines the battle-worthiness of a man or divinity, means anything other than its Vedic equivalent *śúra-* "mighty," and there is no reason to suppose it is a fossil word whose etymological affiliation with *sū* has been forgotten. *zauuanō.sū-*, an epithet applied to gods in general (Ny.3.11) and to Apạm Napāt in particular (Yt.19.52), can not have the meaning "der auf Anruf, wenn gerufen, hilft," as Bartholomae (1904, col. 569) proposes: this compound-syntax is impossible. But if the meaning "who prospers" is given the second term, *°sū-*, the compound can be explained quite naturally. The first term does not represent the Vedic *hávana*, "call," but its homonym "libation," used in the normal instrumental function. *zauuanō.sū-* means "who prospers by way of the libations" (Kellens, 1974, pp. 102-103). Therefore, given the meaning of the root from which it is derived, *sauua(h)-* can not mean "profit" or "salvation," but designates a sort of physical robustness—the most exact translation is "opulence"—attained by means of the sacrificial path (43.3 *sauuaŋhō paθō* "the paths of opulence") that *rādah* "success in ritual" opens between the worshipper and the divinity.

---

17 Smith and Insler: "salvation," Duchesne-Guillemin: "salut," Lommel: "Heil." In the last years of the nineteenth century, a violent debate opposed the "traditional" school (Spiegel, Darmesteter), who maintained that Avesta could only be understood in the light of indigenous commentaries, to the "Vedic" school (Geldner, Bartholomae) who intended to favor comparisons with Vedic texts. It is worthwhile noting, to shed light on Bartholomae's change of opinion on the meaning of *sauua(h)-*, that it was in the interval between the publication of the *Grundriss* (1896) and the *Altiranisches Wörterbuch* (1904) that he learned Pahlavi.

Bartholomae (1904, col. 1291) translates *yāh-* by "Krise, Entscheidung, Wendepunkt."[18] This hypothesis makes it necessary to declare the etymology of the word unknown.[19] However, to all evidence, *yāh-* is an abstract derivation, ending in *-h-*, of the root *yā* (= Ved. *yā: yáti*), which means "to go (by other means than on foot)," or "to request" (Humbach, 1952, p. 18). Using the first meaning, H. P. Schmidt (1968, pp. 177-178) gives the translation "track" and Monna (1978, p. 197) "pilgrimage"; referring to the second meaning and, after a detailed analysis of several passages of Young Avestan, Kuiper (1960, pp. 250-251) sees in *yāh* the "verbal contest." Humbach tries to unify the two meanings of the verb by translating "Bittgang," and I myself have tried to combine Humbach's and Kuiper's interpretations by proposing "formulation oratoire de la demande" (1974, pp. 130-132). The difficulty lies in the fact that, although the etymology of the word is obvious, the base root has two divergent meanings, and the extant contexts, obscure or of little significance, do not permit further clarification of the etymological lessons. The passages from the Young Avesta indicate indisputably that *yāh-* is closely associated with the use of speech, perhaps the art of oratory. Although the situation is much less clear in the *Gāθās*,[20] Y.46.14 makes it possible to propose a hypothesis. This stanza begins with a question addressed to Zarathustra, which says approximately: "who is your ally?" and ends with a phrase ("I call those who ...") that indeed seems to introduce the three following stanzas, which enumerate by name the most eminent members of the Gathic community, addressing advice to them or asking them to take a stand. Between these two movements is inserted the phrase

---

18 With Geldner (1889, p. 24). Then Smith: "(great) judgment," Duchesne-Guillemin: "grande épreuve," Lommel: "Wende, Entscheidung," Insler: "retribution."

19 Some, after Hertel (1925, p. 143), tried to explain *yāh-* by *yah* "to boil," basing their reasoning on the fact that the last judgment in Pahlavi books contained a trial by molten metal. But how to accept a neuter root-noun with unchanging long degree, from this root?

20 Translating by "request" seems to fit and to satisfy the attestation of *Yasna Haptaŋhāiti* Y.36.2-3 ... *nå mazištāi yåŋhąm paitī.jamiiå ātarš vōi mazdå ahurahiiā ahī* "May you meet our greatest request, for you are the fire of Ahura Mazdā."

aṱ huuō kauuā vīštāspō yāhī
  "the Kavi Vīštāspa has arrived at the moment of *yāh*"

This is not in reply to the initial question, since *aṱ* does not have the function of marking transitions of this type. It indicates that the speaker has stopped questioning and resumes his normal course of speech (Pirart, in Kellens-Pirart, *Les textes vieil-avestiques*, 1981-91, vol. 2, p. 115). It is tempting to conclude that *yāh-* is the name of the verbal act to follow: hailing, challenging.

Bartholomae (1904, col. 1109) does not establish a correspondence between *maga-* and the Vedic *maghá-* "gift/blessing" because the first is masculine and the second, neuter. The translation "Geheimbund," then, is something of a hypothesis.[21] Despite the difference in gender, the equivalence between the Vedic and Old Avestan words is admitted, first by Carnoy (1908), then by Smith ("gift") and by Humbach (1952, pp. 15-24). This position is strengthened by one particular textual parallel: Y.51.16 *tąm ... magahiiā ... nąsaṱ ... yąm cistīm* and Y.53.7 *ahiiā magahiiā ... yaθrā ... anąsaṱ parā* as well as RV.1.151.9 *nanaśur maghám* and RV.5.10.3 *maghā́ny ānaśúḥ* make *maghá-/maga-* dependent on the verb *naś/nas*.[22] The use of *maga-* in the masculine is verifiable only in Y.53.7 *magə̄m tə̄m*, where it can be explained by a play on words:

aṱcā və̄ mīždəm aŋhaṱ ahiiā magahiiā yauuaṱ āžuš zarazdištō būnōi haxtiiå
  paracā mraocąs aorācā ... iuuizaiiaθā magə̄m tə̄m
    "may there be for you reward for this blessing, the same as *āžu* (?) most
    confident plunging in and out of the depths of the thighs ... you shall
    snatch this blessing."

The obvious sexual allusion in this passage makes me think that the second time, *maga-* was given a foreign gender in order to create a confusion with the homonym *maga-* "hole," which is masculine and should be used, as is *ūna-*, also masculine, to designate the female organ.

There is no word in Old Avestan for reward or punishment after death. The hereafter is present: here and there the singer threatens his enemies with

---

21 Duchesne-Guillemin: "sacrement," Lommel: "Bund," Insler: "great task."
22 This parallel has been largely unknown until now because the stem *nāsa-* was attributed to its homonym *nas* "to disappear." The parallel also makes it necessary to review this interpretation.

hell and promises his followers heaven, but that is all. The idea of a last judgment is most certainly absent, and eschatology not only does not play a central role in moral thinking, it has not even produced an abstract specialized vocabulary. The interpretations that have been given to the name of the bridge leading to paradise are an admirable illustration of how eschatology and morality are overrated. The expression *cinuuatō pərətu-* is composed of the name of the bridge (*pərətu-*) and its genitive *cinuuatō*. It is not, then, the "*cinuuat* bridge" as has too often been published, but the "*cinuuant*'s bridge." The present participle *cinuuant-* seems to designate a mythical being not otherwise identified and who does not figure anywhere else. To date, three explanations have been given:

1. Bartholomae (1904, cols. 596-597) connects *cinuuant-* with [1]*ci* (col. 441 [1]*kay* "legere") and translates "Brücke des Scheiders." This would be the sorter's bridge, the bridge of the one who separates the good from the bad.
2. Nyberg (1937, p. 205) invokes *ci* "to notice," well attested in Vedic, and postulates "the scrutinizer's bridge."
3. Bailey (1939, pp. 115-116) bases his translation on [2]*ci* "pay retribution for an error" and proposes "bridge of the exactor."

The three *ci* roots attested in Indo-Iranian have thus been used, and each offers a meaning that might well define the final obstacle separating the soul from heaven. Nevertheless, one decisive grammatical clue makes it possible to choose among the three: *cinuuant-* comes from the present of a verb with a nasal infix: *cinu-*. Nyberg's and Bailey's solutions can therefore be excluded. Although Bartholomae's hypothesis is the only plausible one, it can not be accepted without reservations. The objection can be raised, and Bailey raised it, that "sorter's bridge" is based on the meaning of the verb composed with *vī* and not on the simple form. The latter, to which the meaning of *cinuuant-* necessarily corresponds, is not well attested in Indian and only dubiously in Avestan, but it is found in Western Middle Iranian: Manichean Middle Persian and Parthian have the stem *cyn-*, which can also be found in the Persian verb *cīdan*. The meaning "gather, accumulate" or, precisely, "pile up" is confirmed by Sasanian inscriptions, by the Middle Persian *cyt'k*, Parthian *šyty* < *cītāka* "pile of stones." *cinuuatō pərətu-* can only be "the Piler's bridge." The "Piler" is the one who built the bridge by piling one stone upon another, and can hardly be anyone but Yima, who, in the same manner as he is to build the *vara*, builds the path to paradise. His

Indian counterpart, probably an innovation, is simply "the pathfinder." *cinuuatō pərətu-* contains no moral connotation, but a mythological memory.

The central theme of Old Avestan reflection is therefore not composed of eschatology nor of a systematic opposition between good and evil, which is supposed to be its foundation.

According to which of the major divisions is being considered, the Avesta offers a highly diverse image of Mazdaism: the *Yasna*, the *Yašts*, and the *Videvdad* seem to differ by the nature of their religious systems. The dominant impression is that the *Videvdad* "law of the separation from demons" is the most recent part, but that remains merely an impression, inasmuch as there is no one discernible detail of language that clearly demonstrates that this book is more recent than the others or that it is set down in a particular dialect. This long catalog of religious laws, regulations designed to ensure the ritual purity of everything that was to participate in the liturgy (the site of the cult, the fire, the utensils, the men themselves and what they wore on their bodies), constitutes the canonical testimony on Mazdean dualism as it appears in the Pahlavi books from the Sasanian period, its formation going back to the Achaemenian period.[23] A god of good, associated with light, Ahura Mazdā, and a god of evil, associated with darkness, Aṇgra Maniiu, preside over the universe as a whole, which they have created and where each has forged his own domain. From the beginning, they have been fighting to gain supremacy, and man is obliged to take sides in this contest, which will end in a final crisis.

The *Yašts* contain the most correct and coherent texts of the Young Avestan corpus and it is they that have permitted the relative dating of the Avesta, since the evolution of the language used corresponds *grosso modo* to that of the Old Persian in Achaemenian inscriptions. These hymns to various divinities, of whom the most important are Miθra and Anāhitā, are obviously polytheistic, but it is clearly a polytheism with a dominant god, each particular divinity being subordinate to Ahura Mazdā. From the introduction—which reveals the importance of the problem—the principal

---

23 Mazdean dualism is described by Aristotle in *Peri philosophias* and by Plutarch, who claims his information comes from Theopompus. See Gnoli, 1980, pp. 206-219.

Yašts subtly define this subordination, seeking to establish that the divinity in question, Miθra for instance, is at the same time equal and inferior to Ahura Mazdā. As the latter himself puts it: he created Miθra, but he created him his equal. Thus Miθra, who is equal in might to Ahura Mazdā and has the right to the same sacrifices, is all the same his creation.

The *Yasna*, which is recited during the ceremony of preparation of the haoma, is a collection of litanies, often meaningless and grammatically incorrect. It was probably composed at a late date to serve as a setting for the most venerable text of all: the Old Avestan Sequence. It is the nature of the religious system of this sequence that creates problems. Specialists have never agreed on whether Old Avestan Mazdaism was polytheistic, monotheistic, or dualist. If no agreement has been possible on such an elementary definition, it is because there are arguments for all of the hypotheses. Polytheism? Ahura Mazdā is not alone. Far from it: the first stanza of the hymn begins with: "I ask of all of you ...." Monotheism? Ahura Mazdā occupies a position incomparably more elevated than the other divine beings, none of whose number or function is clearly stated. Dualism? One hymn (Y.30) outlines what seems to be the theory of two spirits, one of whom is at the origin of good, the other, of evil. Western scholarly tradition, from the seventeenth-century travelers in Iran to the great pioneer philologists of the nineteenth century, by way of the protagonists of the eighteenth-century philosophers' quarrel, have been attuned to the monotheistic aspect of Mazdaism. This thesis has continued to dominate and has been most recently expressed by Gherardo Gnoli (1980). For Walter B. Henning (1952), dualism, conceived as a protest against monotheism, marks the originality of the Gathic system. This is a heady thesis, stretching likelihood to its limits: it assumes that the Old Avestan doctrine is already the result of a long and chaotic evolution, in the course of which the Indo-Iranian religion underwent its monotheistic revolution, after which this very monotheism gave rise to dualism. As for the polytheistic thesis, it belongs to the least evolutionistic concept of Iranian religion, which advances that the *Gāθās* already contain all of Mazdaism: thus Mary Boyce (1975, 1982), who holds, for example, that, although the name of Miθra is nowhere in Old Avestan texts, this is accidental ...

The dualist thesis can be excluded from its outset, as it rests essentially on the famous stanza Y.30.3, in which is traditionally recognized the expression of the dual spirit theory.[24]

aṭ tā maniiū pouruiiē yā yə̄mā x^vafə̄nā asruuātəm
manahicā vacahicā šiiaoθanōi hī vahiiō akəmcā
åscā hudåŋhō ərəš vīšiiātā nōiṭ duždåŋhō

The first two verses form two phrases, the enclitic pronoun *hī* indicating by its position that *šiiaoθanōi* is the first word of the second phrase. Since *hī* marks the neuter nominative dual, this can not be the case for *šiiaoθanōi*, which is of necessity a locative singular, like *manahi-cā vacahi-cā*. The first sentence is composed of a main clause and a relative clause: *yā* is a true relative pronoun, since Old Avestan doesn't use the *iḍāfat*. The function of the initial particle *aṭ*, which echoes the beginning of stanza 1, is to indicate that the main verb, which is understood, is the same as in 1, to wit: *vaxšiiā*. *yə̄mā* and *x^vafə̄nā* are objects of *sru* in the middle voice and must be explained in the context of the constructions governed by this verb. It is certain that *yə̄mā* is the predicate noun of the subject required for "être connu comme" (to be known as), but *x^vafə̄nā* can not be an instrumental singular, which would make the meaning "to be known for"; *yə̄mā* and *x^vafə̄nā* are thus both nominative duals. We end up with the following meaning:

> "(je veux proclamer) les deux états d'esprit fondamentaux qui sont connus comme des songes jumeaux lors de la pensée et de la parole; lors de l'acte, il y a les deux (actes): le meilleur et le mauvais. D'entre les deux, les généreux distinguent bien, pas les avares."[25]

Or, to paraphrase: the two states of mind, which are the foundation of ritual conduct on all three of its levels (thought, word, act), are twin dreams in the case of the thought and word. They are dreams because they define the zero

---

24 For the various interpretations, see Gnoli, 1980, pp. 206-219.
25 ["(I wish to proclaim) the two fundamental states of spirit, which are known as twin dreams at the time of the thought and the speech; at the time of the act, there are the two (acts): the better and the bad. Between the two the generous distinguish well, not the misers."]

degree of conduct, which exists on an even lower level than that of the thought,[26] and they are twins because, on the two levels under consideration, they can not easily be distinguished one from the other. It is at the moment of the act that it becomes clear that one inspires the good act, the other the evil one. Unlike good divinities,[27] evil ones make no distinction between the two states of mind and accept the bad ritual as well as the good.

Stanza Y.30.3 does not propound a myth on the origin of good and evil—the verbs are not in the past tense; it outlines an analysis of human behavior perceived in the narrow context of ritual activity. At the same time, it reveals that it is indeed their conception of the ritual that separates the Gathic community from its adversaries, even if it is not possible to see what concrete practices are at stake. It is not the germ of dualism that we see in the *Gāθās*,[28] but the seed of a psychology, caught at the moment the idea of an "existence of thought" *(ahu- manaŋhō)* is as yet impossible to conceive as separate from ritual activity.

There remains the choice between polytheism and monotheism. The situation is as follows: Ahura Mazdā enjoys incomparable prestige and is omnipresent in the text, but is not the sole divine being in the Old Avestan religious scheme. Beside him can be found, not the gods of the Indo-Iranian pantheon from the Vedic or Young Avestan versions, but a group of divine beings traditionally defined as the group of the six *aməša spənta*, or "beneficent immortals." It is significant that Western scholars are reluctant to call them "gods," preferring "entities" ("Wesenheit" in German) or

---

[26] The motif is attested again in Y.34.5 *kā īštiš šiiaoθanāi mazdā yaθā vā hahmī* "What is the sacrificial doctrine, O Mazdā, for the act or for when I sleep?"

[27] *hudāh-* "bounteous" and *duždāh-* "stingy" always designate divine beings.

[28] Although there is no trace in the *Gāθās* of dualism as a religious system, certain aspects evoke it, for example, the systematic opposition of antonyms. Two of the four unquestionable entities are constantly opposed: Aša and Druj, Vohu Manah and Aka Manah. But there is no system in this either: Xšaθra has no opposite and can himself take on a negative value; Ārmaiti has not one, but two antonyms, very rarely attested: *tarō.maiti-* "disdain" and *pairi-maiti-* "omission." Furthermore, mankind is necessarily on the side of the allies or the adversaries, and the latter are mercilessly classed in the camp of the counter-entities.

adopting the indigenous name.[29]   There are two reasons for refusing them full divine status:

1. The names of the first three entities are neuter in gender, and the three others are feminine.
2. The name is primarily an abstract noun that most often functions as such. Personification is only sporadic.

The six entities traditionally considered are, in order of frequency: Aša, Vohu Manah, Xšaθra, Ārmaiti, Hauruuatāt, and Amərətāt (Amərətatāt). French philologists translate Aša by "justice," the Germans by "Wahrheit," diverging translations whose common denominator can be found in the etymological meaning of "the right way of ordering" things. Vohu Manah is "(ritual) good thinking." Xšaθra signifies "power," but this is not, especially in the *Gāθās*, power of a political sort. Humbach gives the following definition (1959, II, p. 86): "es ist die magische Potenz mit der sich der Priester die Gottheit geneigt macht." Ārmaiti is "(ritual) fairmindedness," a way of thinking that does not disdain or neglect, but takes everything fairly into consideration. Hauruuatāt and Amərətāt are, respectively, "wholeness of body, good health" and "immortality."

When it comes to interpreting the structure and meaning of the group, commentators in their vast majority repeat in substance the teachings of the Pahlavi books, for which each entity is the patron and personification of a natural element (Aša: fire, Vohu Manah: the cow, Xšaθra: metal, Ārmaiti: the earth, Hauruuatāt: the waters, Amərətāt: plants). In 1945, Dumézil[30] tried to show that the function of these entities was to express the threefold ideology whose structure had been endangered by the monotheistic reform. According to this theory, Aša and Vohu Manah embodied the two aspects of sovereignty and Xšaθra, the fighting function, while Hauruuatāt and Amərətāt, frequently associated in a *dvandva*-compound, constituted the twin couple in charge of fertility. Ārmaiti was the female entity who transcended all these functions or, one at a time, embodied each.

---

29   In 1945, Dumézil conferred on them the title of Archangel, referring explicitly to the verse of Baudelaire: "l'éternelle fête des Trônes, des Vertus, des Dominations."

30   His analysis is accepted by Duchesne-Guillemin.

The presence of entities has never been a handicap for the thesis of monotheism. Not only do these abstract divinities—occasional and imperfect allegories, somehow asexual—not have a status comparable to Ahura Mazdā; according to an interpretation that reached its acme with Maria Wilkins Smith, greatly influenced Duchesne-Guillemin and can be glimpsed in all research, they are but hypostases of Ahura Mazdā. This hypothesis is founded on a piece of evidence of stylistic order: whereas the name of Ahura Mazdā is never attested in the instrumental case, it is in this case that the entities are most frequently mentioned—but not all of them, and this restriction should have raised questions. When Ahura Mazdā accomplishes an action and the verb expressing this action is accompanied by the instrumental form of the names of Aṣa, Vohu Manah or Xšaθra, that would mean that he is acting as Aṣa, as Vohu Manah or as Xšaθra. Seen in this light, the entities would be merely punctual modes of Ahura Mazdā's activity. This interpretation is a postulate. The instrumental form of the entities' names occurs so frequently that it seems abnormal, but it is impossible to show that this denotes an innovative use with respect to ordinary Indo-Iranian syntax. I personally believe that the instrumental case is used frequently because it is the case that gives the name an adverbial function: to act by Aṣa is to act according to the order of things, as it should be, legitimately, even efficiently. If Old Avestan instrumentals are interpreted according to the criteria Delbrück defined for Vedic, which leads to no problems, nothing speaks for seeing the entities as aspects of Ahura Mazdā. They are persons in their own right, who can claim, as does the great god, the title of *ahura* (Y.30.9; Y.31.4) and who are at one with him in a great many elliptic plurals.[31]

It would be impossible to proceed further had not Johanna Narten (1982) recently completely renewed the terms of the problem. At the end of a detailed analysis, she comes to the conclusion that the Gathic entities, far from being represented by the group of the six beneficent immortals alone, which was constituted only in the Young Avesta, form a list that remained open. They can be recognized and counted only by carefully noting the elements of personification scattered throughout the Gathic text. Having

---

31 For example, Y.28.2 *yə̄ vå mazdā ahurā pairijasāi* "I who want to serve you, O Mazdā" means elliptically: "I who want to serve you, O Mazdā (thee and the entities)."

done this, Narten establishes the following carefully nuanced catalog: Aṣa, Vohu Manah and Ārmaiti; "auch" Spəṇta Maniiu and Xšaθra; "gelegentlich" Sraoša and Aṣi; "in Ansätzen" Hauruuatāt and Amərətāt; "vielleicht" Daēnā."[32]   The importance of Narten's work is that it has definitively made obsolete, for the ancient period, all interpretations of the system of entities based on the canonical group of six beneficent immortals and encourages scholars to go fishing for entities. For it is this list that seems most questionable in her work. Narten continues to depend too heavily on the traditional analysis of the functions of the Gathic instrumental. For example, when Ahura Mazdā is the subject of the verb "to come," accompanied by an abstract noun in the instrumental case, Narten assumes the instrumental is used as a comitative and concludes that the abstract noun is personified. This interpretation is not obvious: 43.4 $\theta\beta\bar{a}$ *maniiū ... jasō* for example, does not necessarily mean "you come with your *maniiu*," but may mean "you come with the help of or because of your *maniiu*." If strict criteria for personification are retained, accepting only the use of the vocative and inclusion in a family metaphor, Aṣa, Vohu Manah, Xšaθra and Ārmaiti are the only unquestionable entities. In the discussion on whether the entities compromise the monotheistic thesis, it is possible and even wise to keep to this hard core.[33] From Aṣa to Xšaθra, by way of

---

[32] *spəṇta maniiu* "the beneficent state of mind," *sraoša* "religious discipline," *daēnā* "religious conscience."

[33] Doubtlessly it can not be claimed that the list of entities is complete with those four, but no other plays a comparable role. I can not analyze here the status and function of several "more-or-less entities" that I would divide into five categories:

1. Entities by association, like *aṣi-*, *hauruuatāt-*, *amərətāt-*, *utaiiūiti-* "youth," and *təuuīšī-* "tonus," who are personified only because they are towed along in the wake of a principal entity, especially Ārmaiti, whose gender they share.

2. Virtual entities, like *ādā-*, *īžā-* "offrande" (offering) and *āzūiti-* "libation," for whom nothing says they can not attain personification as do their Vedic equivalents.

3. Metonymic entities, like *sraoša-* and *daēnā-*, who embody one aspect of the religious soul of the sacrificer.

4. Genies or guardian spirits like *gə̄uš tašan* "the maker of the cow," who gives the impression of being a secondary god whose intervention, in Y.29, in favor of the cow shows he is excluded from the rank of gods who decide, but can intervene and suggest.

Vohu Manah, a subtle grading can be seen in frequency of occurrence, personification and association with the name of Ahura Mazdā. It is a far cry from Aṣa, who occasionally figures as a true divinity, to Xšaθra, who is only rarely personified. The three neuter entities who obey this implicit hierarchy have in common their inactivity: they occur rarely as subjects and when they do, it is only of the verb "to be." They are thus distinct from the female entity Ārmaiti, more rarely mentioned than Xšaθra, but who is always personified and who can, as Ahura Mazdā himself, be the subject of a verb of action. Ahura Mazdā then appears as a divinity whose rank is above comparison, surrounded by at least four entities whose frequency of intervention and degree of activity are all unequal. Their inferiority with respect to Ahura Mazdā results in four objective traits: they are mentioned less frequently; personification is unstable; they are sexually inferior; they are used in family metaphors, Aṣa and Vohu Manah becoming the sons of Ahura Mazdā and Ārmaiti, his daughter.

The *daēuuas* are other divine persons of the Gathic religious universe. Their name corresponds to the title *(devá-)* carried by Indian gods in accordance with the Indo-European legacy (**deiu̯ó-* > Lat. *deus*, etc.) and finally comes to designate the anonymous demons of later Mazdaism. The *Gāθās* are precious in that they are situated at the beginning of the current of unpopularity which was to affect this category of divinities. They bear witness to a time of conflict. The religious struggle against the *daēuuas* and their followers is obviously the order of the day, and an entire hymn (Y.32) is devoted to enumerating reproaches made them. The hymn reveals five essential facts:

1. The first stanza divulges that the *daēuuas* and their followers recognize Ahura Mazdā's authority and ask favors of him through sacrifices. This means that the adversaries of the Gathic community are also Mazdean inasmuch as, although they offer a cult to the gods of the pantheon, they believe in the preeminence of Ahura Mazdā.

2. The eighth stanza reveals that, in the past, the Gathic community also honored the *daēuuas*. It may be deduced that, on the one hand, the Gathic community is at the root of a religious innovation, and, on the other, that the *daēuuas*, whose name is never pronounced, are indeed the traditional

---

5. Sacred living beings, essentially cattle in general under the name of *gə̄uš uruuan-* "soul of the cow" and Zarathustra as *nā spəṇtō* "beneficent man."

gods of the Indo-Iranian pantheon. It can not be otherwise, since the expressions *daēuuā vīspåŋhō* and *daēuuāišcā mašiiāišcā* correspond respectively to the Vedic *víśve devāḥ* "all the gods" and *devá mártya* "gods and men."

3.   The followers of the *daēuuas* are situated at a specific level of the social organization; Iranian tradition distinguishes four circles of social belonging, each of which is larger than the preceding: *x͘aētu-* "family," *vīs-* "clan," *airiiaman-* "tribe," *daχiiu-* "nation." It is clear that the chiefs of the *daχiiu-* are the enemy *par excellence* (see also Y.46.1). Those who sacrifice to the *daēuuas* are designated in the third stanza, as in a few other passages, by the title *maz* "great," which defines a master of temporal power.

4.   The main criticism the Gathic community makes of the *daēuuas* seems to be of a ritual order. The *daēuuas* make no distinction between the good and bad state of mind which, for the faithful, determines the choice of sacrificial conduct (Y.30.3-6). This being the case, they accept the homage of a bad ritual. It must be carefully understood that the *daēuuas* were not considered malevolent in an elementary way. When they are qualified as *duš.šiiaoθna-* "of bad acts," that does not mean that they perform bad actions, but that they are offered bad ritual acts. In the same manner, if they are *duš.xšaθra-* "of bad power," that does not mean that they are bad masters, but that the ritual charm their followers use on them is not legitimate.

5.   The Gathic community criticizes the ritual appreciated by the *daēuuas* for being characterized by *aēnah* (= Ved. *énas*), a term which signifies, in the strict sense "l'acte de violence" (act of violence), and in a looser sense: "la faute, le manquement" (fault, failure). Hymn Y.32 gives examples, of which several are incomprehensible. It appears that *aēnah* is used in both ritual and economic activity. From the ritual standpoint, the followers of the *daēuuas* are accused of blunting the power of the hymns (9). We are told that they pronounce a bad hymn "to see by themselves the cow and the sun," which could mean that the nocturnal nature of their ritual is disapproved of (10). They are accused of setting ablaze the trickles of haoma and of mistreating the cow to put her to death, which is the same as disapproving the use of intoxicating liquors and cruel forms of animal sacrifice (14). From an economic standpoint, they are criticized for blunting the means of subsistence (11): they ravage pastures (10) and are perhaps opposed to a fair sharing of the reserves (11).

How is the religious conflict between the Gathic community and the followers of the *daēuuas* translated in concrete terms? It is only known that the latter reproach the Gathic priest for preventing their seeing Aša (Y.32.13), that is, for not ensuring them the benefit of ritual success and, sometimes, for forcing them to practice *aēnah* (Y.46.7)—all this makes sense only if the Gathic sacrificer is occasionally in the service of the followers of the *daēuuas*. The disagreement did not stop with theological disputes and verbal excesses: this seems indicated by Y.32.10, which states that the follower of imposture raises his arm against the follower of Aša. There is, however, no conclusive evidence of an armed conflict. It may be that the Gathic community, visibly in an inferior position, may have undergone more or less violent coercion in the area of religious practices.

Coming back to the central question: does the presence of entities and the *daēuuas* invalidate the thesis of monotheism? It has been seen that even the most important entities could not be put on the same level as Ahura Mazdā. As for the *daēuuas*,[34] hymn 32 dictates a nuanced description of their status: they are neither demonized nor rejected nor frankly condemned; they are criticized for letting their followers commit *aēnah* in offering their cult (32.3, 4). finally, Ahura Mazdā finds himself side-by-side with some gods who are not yet really gods and with others who are already no longer gods, but all have their place in the religious sphere. The *Gāθās* bear witness to a time of crisis in the history of one religion. For reasons which are most probably of a social order, as Antoine Meillet emphasized (1925), questions are raised about certain ritual practices, and the criticism extends to the divinities who receive homage, the preeminent god excluded, in the exclusive cult from which the opponents are seeking refuge. The gods produced by allegory are candidates for the positions of the *daēuuas* made vacant when they fell into disfavor. Whatever may have happened next,[35] polytheism was renewing its personnel. The religious system depicted by the *Gāθās* corresponds to a specific moment in history. It is because the

---

[34] The *daēuuas* are not the only negative divinities in the *Gāθās*. The counter-entities (cf. n. 31) must be taken into consideration, as well as a few evil forces, like *aēšma-*, for which I have difficulty in evaluating their degree of personification.

[35] The Gathic doctrine must have undergone a certain evolution: the *Yasna Haptaŋhāiti*, from which the *daēuuas* are absent, is a text which seems situated far from all conflict.

phenomenon is imminently transitory that neither the word polytheism nor monotheism can provide a satisfying definition. If I had really to choose between the two, I would emphasize the historical perspective and suggest that Old Avestan Mazdaism be defined as an unstable polytheism.

Achaemenid Religion: Preliminary Questions (1987)

NONE OF THE PARTICIPANTS in the workshop on "Sources for the Iranian religion in the Achaemenid period" has taken up the old question about the Zoroastrianism of the Achaemenids, for the good reason that the organizers had asked them not to! I beg you to excuse one of the organizers for breaking his own ban, in order to justify himself. Indeed, I think an explanation is in order, all the more so because I have myself on various occasions until quite recently taken up this subject,[1] and I should explain the reasons for what may well look like a complete turn-about.

Clarisse Herrenschmidt's and my decision was based on the conviction that it is no longer possible to discuss this subject the way it was still legitimate to do so ten years ago. Since then, our knowledge about Mazdaism has been profoundly shaken,[2] and, among other things, almost all of us now favor a different chronology of its history. Clearly, the question of the Zoroastrianism of the Achaemenids is a real question only if one makes Zarathustra a contemporary with Cyrus—which, in practice, amounts to trusting the tradition which places him 258 years before Alexander. As soon as one postulates a distance of 300-400 years between Zarathustra and the founding of the Achaemenid empire, the case is closed, as both Gherardo Gnoli and myself pointed out independently and in the same year,[3] although we do not see eye-to-eye over the origins of Mazdaism. If the OAv. Mazdaism arose around 1000 B.C.E. as a radical upheaval of the religious thought, three hypotheses on its situation in the 6th century are theoretically possible. (1) it had impregnated the entire Iranian religion; (2) it had disappeared in the sands of the salt desert; (3) it had been imperfectly

---

1   "Die Religion der Achämeniden," 1983, pp. 107-123 (German translation of an inaugural lecture held at Liège in 1980).

2   Note especially Narten, 1982, 1986.

3   Gnoli, 1980, pp. 199-206; Kellens, "Die Religion der Achämeniden," 1983, p. 123.

propagated, installing itself lastingly in a relationship of conflict with the persistent "paganism." The simple fact that its liturgical texts (*Gāθās* and *Yasna Haptaŋhāiti*) have been preserved excludes no. (2), and no. (3) is not probable, as there appears to be no substantial religious crisis throughout Achaemenid history, a fact that was noticed long ago. In the framework of the long chronology, which is today almost universally accepted, the Achaemenid Zoroastrianism is necessarily a post-Zoroastrian Mazdaism, like that of the Young Avesta, even though it may not be the same.

The question: were the Achaemenids Zoroastrian or not? is suspect for still another reason: the elusiveness of the term "Zoroastrian." Can one seriously ask whether a religious doctrine is "Zoroastrian" or not without a rigorous definition of the term?[4] Most scholars do not even begin to define the term, by saying whether they mean the doctrine of the entire Avesta or only of those parts that seem to have been composed during Zarathustra's lifetime, the parts that we today define as Old Avestan. From Benveniste (1929), the backbone of discussions on the Achaemenid religion was a list of "omissions and divergences," but today it is no longer a justifiable method to include, for example, *both* the omission of the exclusively YAv. title *yazata and* the omission of the Amǝša Spǝntas, which used to be regarded as an essential and indisputable characteristic of the Gathic doctrine.[5] We are not only dealing with a flaw in the perspective, an unavoidable consequence of the short chronology, but simply a flaw in the methodology. As soon as one notices divergences between the religious systems of the Old and Young Avesta, whatever the chronology one adopts, one must carefully give to each what belongs to it.[6] It is self-evident that the long chronology, independently of what it implies from a general point of view, compels us to consider the question of the Zoroastrianism of the Achaemenids only by reference to the OAv. corpus, for, although the Achaemenid documents may not be earlier than the entire Young Avesta,

---

4 As clearly seen by Duchesne-Guillemin, 1972, pp. 76-77.

5 Today, after Narten's work, this situation has been reversed, as *yazata* is used in the *Yasna Haptaŋhāiti*, which we now know is an OAv. text, and the Gathic Entities are neither called *amǝša spǝnta* nor do they form a closed list.

6 As does Ilya Gershevitch, despite adhering to the short chronology (1964, pp. 12-16), who distinguishes carefully between Gathic "Zarathustrianism," YAv. "Zarathustricism," and Sasanian "Zoroastrianism."

they are definitely earlier than some of it (which is why the funerary practices, for instance, are irrelevant).

The question is so difficult to answer because we really know so little about OAv. Mazdaism. All those who discuss the Zoroastrianism of the Achaemenids do so with an implicit idea of what exactly the originality of the Gathic system was. But they all have a different idea, for no consensus has ever been reached regarding the criteria for defining OAv. Mazdaism. Is it dualism? Gnoli has showed—conclusively, I think—that this is not the case.[7] Is it monotheism? I recently gave my reasons for doubting it,[8] and Mary Boyce, who probably does not believe in mine, has given other reasons,[9] which I do not believe in. Is it Ahura Mazdā's preeminence? It can not be confirmed. Is it the invention of the Aməša Spəntas? It can no longer be assumed, after Johanna Narten's work. Is it the ethics? Let us be serious. Is it anti-ritualism? The *Gāθās*, as interpreted by Humbach—the best interpretation available—bear witness to a rigorously ritualistic doctrine. Is it the rejection of certain practices, such as the bloody sacrifice and the consumption of *haoma*? Scholars have been skeptical on this point for years,[10] which is reasonable, since there are only a couple of incomprehensible allusions to these points in the *Gāθās*. We must resign ourselves to the fact that we have not been able to identify any distinctive feature of OAv. Mazdaism, which is the only one that one might, if one insists, call "Zoroastrianism." There are the *daēuuas*, but that is a useless criterion from a practical point of view, since we know of no religious trend in Iran in which the gods are called *daēuuas*, and since we also do not know who the Gathic *daēuuas* are, one can not use the presence of Miθra or other gods beside Ahuramazdā in the Achaemenid domain as an argument.

To ask about the Zoroastrianism of the Achaemenids is to propose implicitly the confrontation between a poorly known entity: the Achaemenid religion, and—as commonly assumed—a less poorly known entity: Zoroastrianism. I am afraid the situation is the opposite, however, namely that we know the Achaemenid religion better than Zoroastrianism. To tell the truth, our knowledge of OAv. Mazdaism is so incomplete that the validity of the question about the Zoroastrianism of the Achaemenids is

---

7   Gnoli, 1980, pp. 191-192.
8   Kellens, "Characters," 1987, pp. 249-250 [= above pp. 14ff.].
9   Boyce, 1975, pp. 195-196.
10 See Humbach, 1977, pp. 17-29.

uncertain, at best. For this question obviously only makes sense if Zoroastrianism really exists, that is, a religious doctrine that was:

1. so radically innovating that it would have conflicted with the preexisting religion,
2. a work of an individual, established and preached by a powerful historical personality,
3. propagated by a deliberate and persevering missionary activity.

These are just postulates, which till now, quite astonishingly, have not been questioned more often and more firmly. It is incoherent, not to say absurd, to take for granted the radical character of an innovation that can not be further analyzed. Is the Gathic text so transparent that the role played by Zarathustra in it appears with all the precision we could wish for?[11] Few scholars have avoided the contradiction that consists in proclaiming without hope the irremediable obscurity of the *Gāθās*, then to describe with great confidence the religious system it bears witness to. If we just look at the facts, we see that none of us has been able to go beyond the following evident realization, to which we all subscribe intimately, namely, that the *Gāθās* is a text in the process of being deciphered and which we still hardly understand less than half of. A favorite statement of Gathic scholars is the following of Kaj Barr: "the more I read the *Gāθās*, the less I understand them."[12] They then proceed to explain them by unearthing a meaning that seems to be in harmony with the doctrine one lends them *a priori*, according to a method that Humbach denounced as follows: "Arguments of the type 'it is unclear why the prophet should ...' are common in Gathic studies. Nevertheless, it is doubtful whether they should be used."[13] How many

---

11 Let me add that there is no clear allusion anywhere in the Avesta to proselytizing. The passage cited most often to support this point is Y.42.6 *aθaurunąmcā paitī.ająθrəm ... yōi iieiiąn dūrāṯ ašō.īšō daxiiunąm* "And we worship the return of the priests who might have gone far seeking the Aṣa of the nations" (see Kellens, 1974, pp. 13-16). It takes an unshakable optimism to be certain that "to seek the Aṣa of the nations" means "evangelizing."

12 Duchesne-Guillemin, 1948, pp. 13-14

13 Humbach, 1956, p. 82.

times have we read this supreme argument: "it makes a good sense,"[14] which only means that the argument seems to lead to familiar ideas?[15]

The study of the Mazdean religion has everything to gain by ridding itself of the image of a founder or a prophet. This person, who keeps getting in the way, has nothing but drawbacks. Not only is it, most probably, only a red herring, which would not be so bad—it might give rise to jokes à la Bernard Shaw: 'Zarathustra or somebody else of the same name'—, but it also causes scholarship to be satisfied with what is only a rudimentary explanatory principle. The analysis is thought to have reached its goal when it has situated its object with respect to Zarathustra. The only three relevant questions appear to be: "is this inherited from Indo-Iranian, an invention by the prophet, or a later adaptation?" This is how one discussed the Aməša Spəntas, the Frauuašis, Aši, the eschatology, etc. The problem that a concept poses is regarded as solved once the concept is situated in the elementary dialectic scheme of

> the thesis: pre-Gathic religion, which is attested by no text or monument,
> the antithesis: the religion of the *Gāθās*, which we admit we hardly understand,
> the synthesis: Young Avestan and Achaemenid Zoroastrianism, which leaves us
>   in the air, because we can not define them with respect to the two preceding
>   stages.

The fact that the research, by postulating a founder, has not been able to articulate the various manifestations of Mazdaism in a coherent picture that might receive a relative consensus ought to make us extremely skeptical toward the premises.

If we agree to think of the evolution of Mazdaism as continuous, whatever shocks it may have undergone, and not as distributed throughout three irreductible stages, each in itself motionless, this religion will regain

---

[14] Gershevitch, 1962, p. 368; frequent in Insler; etc.

[15] Gathic terminology is very deceptive in that it seems to use the same idioms as we do, for instance "good thought, good speech, good action" and "the straight road." Naturally, these terms mean something very different from what we understand by them. One may blame Duchesne-Guillemin for having encouraged this kind of confusion in his otherwise eminently readable translation of the *Gāθās*, by systematically using Christian analogy such as: *xšaθra-* "kingdom," *maga-* "sacrament," *spənta-* "holy," etc. The *Gāθās* need a good dash of exoticism.

all the dignity and complexity of its historical development. Can we seriously believe that Iranian religious thought had no other stimulus than the visions of the founder and the perpetual resurgences of the past, devoid of any movement beyond the oscillation between the two poles of "pagan" traditions and "prophetic" innovation? Unencumbered by an overly convenient *deus ex machina*, the study of the origins of Mazdaism would be free to look at the real problems, in the framework of an Indo-Iranian religious dialectology. As for the Achaemenid documentation, rather than being a riddle, it gives us an unexpected chance, being the first direct testimony of Mazdaism and, probably, the one that contains the oldest texts after the Old Avesta. Rather than needing the "Zoroastrian" *Avesta* to illuminate it, it helps us better understand that text. How was the pantheon of the *yašts* constituted? What was the place of fire in the ritual? How were the funerary rituals imposed by the *Videvdad* actually practiced? Achaemenid Mazdaism can teach us a lot about these questions and many others, if only we agree to look at it from another angle than its hypothetical conversion. The procedure that consists in starting with the Achaemenid facts and going toward the Avesta can not be more sterile than the opposite.

Duchesne-Guillemin wrote that "the Achaemenids had a very personal way of being Zoroastrian."[16] A meaningful statement! It is correct because it recognizes the specificity of Achaemenid Mazdaism, unfortunate because it reduces the religious debate to a summary confrontation between the great kings and the prophet, because it expresses a strange surprise, after a century of studies, that the prophetic authority neither stopped time nor made all places the same. The Achaemenid religion had its specific features, common and inevitable, which are the result of a special situation in geography and history and the creative evolution of thought, which belongs to all men.

---

16 Duchesne-Guillemin, 1975, p. 20.

Zarathustra and the Old Avesta

Four Lectures at the Collège de France

(1991)

LECTURE I. THE TEXT

THE 1970S AND 80S were very important for Avestan philology. It is true that our knowledge of the Avesta has not been revolutionized—that is perhaps not yet to be expected—but recent research has changed the perspectives in which we view the various aspects of the Avestan text and consequently has shown us the most suitable methodology for approaching it.

The state of the text

The first change of perspective affects how we establish the text. We now know exactly how far to trust the manuscripts we possess, which represent what we may call the Vulgate. Today, after Karl Hoffmann in three brief articles (1969, 1970, 1971) reconstructed with precise arguments the history of the transmission of the Avesta, everybody has accepted his reconstruction. The then reigning "Andreas theory" has now been definitively discarded. This was a theory proposed by Friedrich-Carl Andreas in 1902, according to which the Vulgate was nothing but the clumsy transcription into a differentiated, phonetic, alphabet of an "Arsacid archetype," recorded in an unknown alphabet similar to that of the Book Pahlavi alphabet, in which the vowels are omitted and several consonants graphically identical. Since then, Avestan philology always had to reckon with the possibility of false vocalization, and, in order to make sure a form was authentic, one first had to imagine how it would have been written in the Arsacid archetype. This principle of reestablishing the Arsacid archetype reigned alone for forty years, until the end of World War II, when it began encountering some skepticism. Yet, twenty years later it had still not given way to a firm theory of the history of the text, and Avestan philology was condemned to proceed in an *ad hoc* manner, without principle and without method.

Karl Hoffmann first of all pointed out the importance of the *Prolegomena* in Karl-Friedrich Geldner's critical edition of the Avesta. In the *Prolegomena* the manuscripts are classed in families and the relationships between the manuscripts clearly established. From the point of view of the "Andreas theory," this work had only very little practical importance, especially in view of the recent date of the manuscripts, which are none of them earlier than the 13th century. Two of the oldest manuscripts containing the oldest part of the Avesta are J_2 and K_5, written by the same scribe and dated 1323.

Moreover, it has been proved conclusively on the basis of mistakes shared by all the manuscripts of the individual text groups (*yasna*, *yašts*, etc.) that they all, without exception, are descended from a common original now lost, which Hoffmann called the "Stammhandschrift" and dated to the 9th-10th centuries of our era. The consequence of this discovery is that on no account can a single manuscript contain a "miracle" reading, that is, a better reading than that of the original 9th-10th-century manuscript. Comparison of the extant manuscripts can only give us the probable reading of this already seriously corrupt original. Thus, we see that not only is the manuscript tradition recent compared to the age of the *Avesta* itself, it is also very tenuous.

The paleographic analysis of the Avestan alphabet shows that it was invented in Sasanian times.[1] The inventor (or inventors?) used two different models. He primarily adopted the signs of the Pahlavi alphabet, a descendant of Aramaic, sometimes modifying them by changing their shapes or adding diacritical marks to express sounds not expressed in the Pahlavi alphabet; he added a few letters taken from an earlier stage of the Pahlavi alphabet known from a fragment of the *Psalms of David* in Middle Persian found in Chinese Turkestan; and occasionally he just made up new letters. Typologically, he applied the principle of "one sign = one sound" of the Latin and Greek alphabets. The use of these two models also furnishes

---

1   [The Sasanian empire lasted from 224 to 651.]

us with some chronological indications. Obviously, the invention of the Avestan alphabet could not have taken place before the Pahlavi alphabet reached the stage reflected in it, which means it could hardly have happened before the beginning of the 5th century. On the other hand, it could hardly have taken place after the fall of the Sasanian empire, since its two models, especially the Greco-Latin one, suggest that it took place in an occidental *ambiance*. The Avestan alphabet was invented for one single purpose, namely, to record the Avesta, and was hardly used for anything else.[2] Its almost obsessive precision is explained by the fact that its purpose was to transcribe exactly the nuances of the solemn liturgical recitation. There is nothing to prove that the *Avesta* had been committed to writing before the Sasanian period. Even if there was an Arsacid archetype or any attempt at committing the *Avesta* to writing by means of a consonant alphabet such as the Middle Persian one, it had no practical influence on the text of the Vulgate, which is derived via the 9th-10th-century original from a lost Sasanian archetype, in which the orally transmitted text was transcribed in the phonetic Avestan alphabet.

We must therefore trust that the orthography of the Vulgate reflects the manner in which it was spoken when it was first reduced to writing. We are not allowed to play around with the vowels, nor those consonants which were once considered interchangeable, such as *r* and *n*. On the other hand, the limitations of the manuscript tradition are also perfectly clear. The text of the Vulgate is corrupt, sometimes profoundly so. It teems with orthographic mistakes, which are, as I pointed out above, sometimes common to all the manuscripts. But by the same token the methodology of Avestan philology is clear. first of all, one must examine the manuscripts employing the classical method of textual criticism. Next, the result of this examination must be confronted with the linguistic postulate. This means one must compare the form won from the examination of the manuscripts with the form we expect from linguistic comparison with the closest relative of Avestan, namely Old Indic (Sanskrit). If there is agreement, we may confidently adopt the reading. If not, uncertainty remains.

It is also clear that a long period of oral transmission elapsed between the time the texts were given their final form and when they were written down,

---

2   [The use of the Avestan alphabet to write Pahlavi or even Persian, so-called Pazand, is of relatively modern date.]

more than a millennium in the case of the oldest texts. About this period we know very little and probably never shall learn more, in view of the lack of sources. Only two facts are incontestable. The old part of the *Avesta* was at some stage edited by learned Mazdean priests (scholars)—Hoffmann calls this editing an ortho-epic diascevasis—which means that the text has come down not only interspersed with glosses and didactic notations, but also in the form of a not very systematic *padapāṭha*. Second, because Avestan was not the language of Persia (modern southern Iran), we must conclude that the Avestan tradition must have moved at least once, at an indeterminate time, from its point of origin toward southwestern Iran. As a matter of fact, a number of possible dialect features have been pointed out, which indicate a rather itinerant history. At any rate, the text was changed, be it through priestly/scholarly manipulation, because it was colored by transmitters of the text speaking various dialects, or by natural evolution of the learned pronunciation of the text. This means that the alphabet devised under the Sasanians does not reproduce the phonetic characteristics of what I shall call the "original language," but those of the liturgical pronunciation of the Sasanian clergy. Any reconstruction of the original language is bound to swing between two extremes, which must both be carefully avoided. On one hand, the assumption that all the particularities of the orthography represent phonetic features of the original language would make Avestan a mongrel language—the Andreas theory luckily took precautions against this extreme, which is probably its only positive aspect. On the other hand, elimination of all the orthographic flourishes by regarding them as having merely been caused by rhetorical emphatic recitation of late date would reduce Avestan to some kind of theoretical Proto-Iranian. Emile Benveniste, for instance, fell into this trap when he tried to describe the Avestan phonology.[3] As a matter of fact, it is impossible to describe the phonology of Avestan, because frequently one does not know whether a given feature belonged to the original language or appeared in the course of oral transmission.

finally, it is impossible to situate Avestan precisely among Iranian dialects, which is also one of the reasons why the question of the Avestan homeland has no answer.

---

3   [Beekes's *A Grammar*, 1988, is also a grammar of Proto-Avestan (Iranian).]

The chronology of the text

The second change in perspective is that of chronology and therefore concerns the situation of the Old Avesta. In the course of the 1970s, with some important exceptions, the specialists one after another adopted a "long chronology" of the text. This implies a return to the hypothesis proposed about 1900 by two great pioneers: Friedrich-Carl Geldner and Christian Bartholomae. According to the long chronology, the old part of the *Avesta* should be placed around 1000 B.C.E. and the younger parts in the Achaemenid period, contemporary with the Old Persian inscriptions. The proposed dates are of course approximate and only have value as points of reference; thus, the long chronology is also a *relative* chronology. The basis for this theory consists of two observations, largely impressionistic, which does not, however, mean they are illusory. On one hand, the degree of evolution of Old Persian and Young Avestan is relatively identical, while, on the other hand, there can on no account be less than two centuries between Old Avestan and the linguistic stage represented by Young Avestan and Old Persian.

This fact has been overshadowed for over fifty years by the concurring positions taken by two scholars of considerable authority, Antoine Meillet in 1925 and Walter B. Henning in 1951. Meillet and Henning opposed Geldner and Bartholomae's long chronology, using the argument that languages develop at different pace. This is a legitimate and theoretically correct argument, but, in this particular case, it is not quite acceptable, because it was used to support a doubtful non-linguistic fact, namely the tradition of the Sasanian clergy that Zarathustra lived 258 years before Alexander. The historians may defend or criticize the value of the Mazdean tradition, but they can certainly not prove it is authentic. In that case, to the linguists, who note that Young Avestan is obviously far more developed than Old Avestan, the traditional date of the Mazdean tradition is bound to be suspect, and to base the chronology of the text on it means putting the chariot before the horse. It is a great paradox that it was two great linguists who did this. It is still more incomprehensible that the argument of the different pace of development of languages remained the only argument of the opponents of the long chronology, because what one did innocently in 1925 and 1951 can no longer be done in the 1990s. In the late 1950s three particularly archaic features of Old Avestan were brought to light, two of which are archaic even by Vedic standards, and which Meillet and Henning did not know when they contested the long chronology:

1. The accusative and the dative-genitive of the enclitic pronouns of the 1st and 2nd plural coalesce in Young Avestan (*nō, vō*), as well as in Vedic (*naḥ, vaḥ*); in Old Avestan, however, the two are still distinguished: the accusative forms are *nå, vå* with originally long vowels (< **nāh/*vāh* < **nās/*vās*), as in Latin (*nōs, vōs*), but the dative-genitive forms are *nō, vō* with originally short vowels (< **nah/*vah* < **nas/*vas*). This linguistic fact could not be properly appreciated till after the Andreas theory was rejected.

2. The structure of the Old Avestan verbal system became fully known only after the analysis of Helmut Humbach (1959). In Old Avestan the present tense is constantly and consistently opposed to the aorist in such a way that all the verbal forms are distributed fairly evenly between the two categories, while Old Persian and Young Avestan almost exclusively use the present.[4] Since all the Iranian dialects must originally have had this system (which comparative linguistics has proved is inherited from the Indo-European proto-language), the old system did not change into the new one overnight. A large number of syntactic distinctions had to be abandoned, not only all those assumed by the aorist, but also many in which the present tense was involved. The aorist became obsolete, and all the verbal categories were regrouped into the single framework of the present tense. In brief, between the Older Avesta and the Younger Avesta, the verbal system evolved from a system of opposing aspects to one of tenses. How could this change have occurred overnight or even in the course of one century?[5]

3. In a series of articles published from 1957 onward, F.B.J. Kuiper showed that numerous metrical irregularities in the *Gāθās* were removed if one assumed that the intervocalic hiatus left after the disappearance of the Indo-European laryngeals remained intact. For instance, the injunctive *dāṯ* < **dheə₁-t* is monosyllabic in the *Gāθās* and thus stands in opposition to the disyllabic subjunctive *dāṯ* < **da'at* < **dheə₁-et*. This feature is of great importance for the chronology of the Avestan texts. It not only highlights the remarkably archaic character of Old Avestan, it also once and for all denounces the frequently-voiced idea that some Young Avestan passages might in fact be older than the Old Avesta itself. The passages in

---

4   [Kellens, *Le verbe*, 1984, pp. 431-433.]

5   [Seen from a different perspective, how could the ancient system have remained virtually intact for over a millennium?]

question have all preserved more or less faithfully the octosyllabic metrical scheme, and it is quite clear that we find no examples of hiatus resulting from ancient laryngeals. Therefore, this old idea is, I believe, no more than an illusion.

The fact that about four centuries separate Old and Young Avestan invites us to restore a terminology that reflects both the uncertainty and the differences of opinion. Old and Young Avestan can be characterized in two different ways: they are different dialects or belong to different stages of linguistic evolution or, even, both. Thus, the language of the Old Avesta is commonly called "Gathic" after the *Gāθās*, underscoring the special dialect, while the language of the Young Avesta is commonly termed "Young(er) Avestan," stressing the chronological difference from Old Avestan. Some years ago, however, Johanna Narten began using "Old Avestan" instead of "Gathic." This was a good choice, because "Old Avestan" has three advantages: it contrasts symmetrically with "Young Avestan," it ratifies explicitly the diachronic reality, and it embraces the remaining texts of the Old Avesta. For, as we shall see, the *Gāθās* are not the only Old Avestan texts, and a more comprehensive term is therefore necessary. This new terminology should not, however, make us forget that Old and Young Avestan are also, in fact, different dialects, so that Young Avestan is not the direct descendant of Old Avestan. For instance, in Old Avestan the pronominal adjective *vīspa-* "all" is declined as an adjective, not as a pronoun, e.g., nom. plur. *vīspåŋhō*, whereas in Young Avestan *vīspa-*, as well as *aniia-* "other," preserves the original pronominal ending *-e* (< *-ai*): *vīspe, aniie*.

I mentioned earlier that the question about the Avestan "home" has no answer. The main reason is that the term "home" has no meaning for a book that contains texts of such divergent age and origin. Rather than "home," we might indeed speak of "travelers' motels." As for the Old Avesta, its age alone prevents us from addressing the question of where it was composed. This took place long before an Assyrian clay tablet mentioning the Parsuwas (835 B.C.E.) provided us with the first testimony for the historical existence of Iranians. Which were the Iranian tribes at such a remote period? where were they? and how differentiated were their respective dialects? Clearly those questions have no answers.

The importance of the chronological gap between the Old Avesta and the Young Avesta should make us doubly skeptical toward the Mazdean traditions of the Sasanian period. At the end of the last century two schools confronted one another: on one hand, the "traditional" school, which attempted to throw light on the Avesta with the help of the indigenous commentaries, more specifically the Pahlavi translations, and, on the other hand, the "Vedicizing" school, which favored comparison with Old Indic (Sanskrit). This ancient quarrel has long since yielded to a relative agreement among specialists. The evidence of the Sasanian school is reliable and precise for a text such as the *Widēwdād* (*Videvdad, Vendidad*), but completely useless for both the Old Avesta and the oldest parts of the Young Avesta. By the Sasanian period, not only the language but also the concepts enshrined in these texts had been either forgotten or profoundly reinterpreted. It is important to realize that the basic vocabulary of the Old Avesta—words such as *maga-* and *yāh-*—had no descendants in Pahlavi and the translator used only calques to render them. We now know, however, that the Sasanian period is not the only one to blame. Even in the sacerdotal passages of the Young Avesta, deficient knowledge of the Old Avesta is evident, which reveals a long evolution of the religious thought, which can only be reasonably accommodated within the framework of the "long chronology." The exegetes of the commentaries interpret wrongly several Old Avestan passages. The most significant example is the *Yeṅhē hātąm* prayer, which is actually a rewriting of the Gathic strophe Y.51.22, based on an erroneous syntactic analysis. The tradition may have been broken, although we have no proof that it was; more probably what we see is the result of modifications that changed the tradition not only between the Avestan and Sasanian Mazdaism, but also between the *Old* and Young Avesta. The testimonies of the Young Avesta and the later tradition concerning the Old Avesta should therefore not be given simple credit and can never count more than the internal analysis of the text, however troublesome it may be.

There is no doubt that Old Avestan is an Iranian language, as it presents the four characteristic features that distinguish the Iranian languages from Indian: merger of the voiced stops and the voiced aspirated stops (*b* and *bh* > *b*, etc.), loss of laryngeals between consonants (*zaotar-* vs. OInd. *havitar-*), change of *s* > *h* in initial and intervocalic position (*ahura-* vs. OInd. *asura-*), and the development of Indo-Iranian **tst, *dzdh* > *st, zd* (*dastē, dazdī* vs. OInd. *datte, daddhi*). But it is also such an archaic language and so isolated by its own archaism that it partly transcends the study of Iranian languages. Not only is it possible to use, without major adjustments, the great works of reference of Indian grammar, but Old Indic scholars are increasingly realizing that it is a necessary complement to their own studies. In several recent works, the Vedic and Old Avestan facts have therefore necessarily been combined. In fact, the study of these two languages implies a kind of hybrid discipline, the special nature of which is clearly illustrated by the title of the *opera minora* of Karl Hoffmann: *Aufsätze zur Indoiranistik.*

The Old Avesta

The third change of perspective derives from our present knowledge that the Old Avesta is not limited to the *Gāθās* alone, which in itself is enough to justify the substitution of the term "Old Avestan" for "Gathic." The situation is the following. About one third of the Vulgate consists of the *Yasna*, and in the middle of the *Yasna* are located the five *Gāθās*, each characterized by a specific meter and arranged in decreasing order according to length. The first three are composed of several chapters, called *hāiti*, each *hāiti* consisting of a variable number of strophes (15 in average). Within this metrical corpus, between the first and the second *Gāθā*, a collection of prose texts is located, the *Yasna Haptaŋhāiti*, which owes its name to the fact that it is composed of seven *hāitis*. The Avestan book of the *Yasna* therefore resembles a double box. The chapters in Young Avestan form a box for the metrical Old Avestan texts, the *Gāθās*, which in turn form a casket for the Old Avestan prose text, the *Yasna Haptaŋhāiti*.

The *Yasna Haptaŋhāiti* is written in the same Old Avestan as the *Gāθās*. This was shown conclusively in an exhaustive study devoted to this text by Johanna Narten (1986). It is still too early for the book to have caused much discussion, and we do not yet know to what extent Narten's conclusions will be accepted. Nevertheless, it seems to me that it will be impossible to contest her demarcation of the text:

1.   It is a prose text, which from a stylistic point of view distinguishes it from the *Gāθās*.

2. It goes from Y.35.2 to the end of *hāiti* Y.41 (the phrase making up Y.35.1 and the *hāiti* Y.42 are additions in Young Avestan, as is Y.52, which is inserted between the last two *Gāθās*, Y.51 and Y.53).

3. Not a single feature of the language in which it is composed hints that it might be older or later than that of the *Gāθās*.

The last point confirms once and for all the two facts that I have already alluded to: that it is useless to look for passages in the *Avesta* that might be older than the Old Avesta and that neither the *yašts*, because of their metrical systems, nor the *Yasna Haptaŋhāiti*, in spite of what the first editor, Theodore Baunack thought, contain pre-Old Avestan texts. It is also useless to look for texts linguistically intermediate between the *Gāθās* and the Young Avesta. The *Yasna Haptaŋhāiti*, to which such a role has generally been assigned, is linguistically not a more recent text than the *Gāθās*. Instead, together they make up the Old Avesta, from which the Young Avesta is separated by a time gap of several centuries, causing a break in the known tradition.

As soon as we admit that the *Yasna Haptaŋhāiti* is an Old Avestan text, the consequences pile up. I shall mention three important ones, before which even Narten seems to have withdrawn, but which I would like to formulate with complete clarity:

1. The first is of a general nature and can not leave Old Indic scholars indifferent. We must now admit that the practice of "art prose" is not an Indic innovation. The fact that the *Avesta* contains an old part composed according to syntactic techniques and style analogous to the *Brāhmaṇa*s forces one to postulate the existence of Indo-Iranian prose, in the same way one postulates, because of the *Gāθās*, the existence of Indo-Iranian poetry.

2. The language of the Old Avesta is not homogeneous. Narten would like to classify the differences observable between the *Gāθās* and the *Yasna Haptaŋhāiti* as purely rhetorical and caused by the difference between prose and verse. But, even if this were all there is to the contrast between the two texts, still one could not completely ignore it, as one strophe (Y.46.17) explicitly attacks the liturgical use of prose. There is thus a difference between the two texts that can not be removed. It may be rhetorical, but even so it is difficult to explain all the linguistic differences between the texts. It is true that they are so minute that one hesitates to talk about two dialects. Perhaps it is better just to admit the existence of

jargons belonging to two different schools. The most noticeable difference is seen in the system of pronominal deixis, where "this" is expressed in the *Gāθās* by the stem *i-*, but in the *Yasna Haptaŋhāiti* by *ima-*, as in Vedic. Some other details: the verb *varz-* "to do" forms a root aorist in the *Yasna Haptaŋhāiti*, but an *s*-aorist in the *Gāθās*; the conjunction that corresponds to Vedic *yávat* is *yauuat* in the *Gāθās*, but *yāt* in the *Yasna Haptaŋhāiti*; the word for "sky," which seems to have been affected by taboo in the entire Old Avesta, has been replaced by *nabah-* "cloud" in the *Gāθās*, but by *raocah-* "light" in the *Yasna Haptaŋhāiti*. That is all, but in such a small text it is considerable. I would therefore recommend that for the sake of precision one should distinguish between Gathic and Haptahatic Old Avestan.

3.   The religious doctrine of the Old Avesta reflects its language: it is imperfectly uniform. Either we are looking at Mazdaism for the first time, at a moment of its development when it was already represented by several schools, or it was not shaped under the conditions we thought we knew. Admittedly, the fundamental differences between the *Gāθās* and the *Yasna Haptaŋhāiti* are not radical; nevertheless, there are two extremely significant ones:

1. Different from that of the *Gāθās*, the atmosphere of the *Yasna Haptaŋhāiti* is perfectly serene; there is no allusion either to a conflict or to enemies.

2. The *Gāθās*, for no discernible reason, are alternately spoken by a single "I" or several "we's"; the *Yasna Haptaŋhāiti*, however, knows only "we," and, incidentally, neither Zarathustra nor anybody else is mentioned by name. Thus the anonymous "we" of the *Yasna Haptaŋhāiti* stands in stark contrast to the star actor of the *Gāθās*, either an authoritative "I" or a consecrated and duly named person.

Nevertheless, Narten is sorely tempted to attribute both texts to the same author, that is, Zarathustra, but the argument she deploys to support this hypothesis does not hold together. It is natural, she says, that the author does not mention his name in his texts. That means that Zarathustra should be considered the author of the *Gāθās* because he is mentioned in them and of the *Yasna Haptaŋhāiti* because he is never mentioned there!

If these differences are not due to separation in time, what is the reason for them?

Even if there were a maximum span of two or three generations between the two texts, how is one to explain the fact that the name of the founder of the religion has totally disappeared and that the so-feared enemy has vanished into thin air? Such an assumption is truly unthinkable, so we have to suppose there were different schools; but as the two schools were close to one another both in space and time, we can not make such a supposition without pondering the role of Zarathustra and the importance and real forms of the conflict apparent in the *Gāθās*. Consequently, we have to reexamine the postulate of a founder and a sudden and radical transformation of the religious thought. This is what we shall do in the next lectures. Today I hope I have shown that in the history of studies the time is now ripe for such a task to be undertaken.

There are still some aspects of the Old Avesta that need to be discussed first, however, as well as of the manner in which the specialists have dealt with it. Differently from the *Yasna Haptaŋhāiti*, which has been the subject of only two major studies, one century apart, namely by Theodor Baunack in 1888 and Johanna Narten in 1986, the *Gāθās* are a veritable best-seller and have been repeatedly visited and commented upon. Since the beginning of this century it has been the object of ten complete studies, five of which are in the form of complete text editions. I see two principal reasons for the fascination the text has for Iranian scholars. The first is the interest, maybe even passion (though one a bit suspect), for the religious system they express. This text, which is reputed to be the work of Zarathustra himself, appears different in content from both the Vedic hymns and the Young Avesta and therefore seems to provide a comfortable confirmation of the prescientific myth of Zarathustra. The second is the beauty of the problem. Here is a short text, relatively faithfully transmitted (much better than the Young Avesta), written in a language which, thanks to comparative Indo-Iranian linguistics, is in principle well known to us, and whose message we are supposed to understand, thanks to the Mazdean tradition and a few Classical testimonies. But we hardly understand it! This paradox is felt as a challenge: there is the mystery of the *Gāθās*, which is what constitutes their allure.

The first phase of "modern" studies reaches from the appearance of C. Bartholomae's *Altiranisches Wörterbuch* in 1904 to Helmut Humbach's first articles in 1952. In this period the paradox took on the following form: there was a practical, objective agreement on the surface meaning of the text, but, in the words of Bernfried Schlerath, "a fascinating discrepancy" regarding the deeper meaning.[6] In this way the main problem of the *Gāθās*

---

6   Schlerath, 1962, p. 567.

appeared as one of exegesis. On the whole, every interpreter, while improving on details, remained dependent upon Bartholomae's grammar of Old Iranian in the *Grundriß der iranischen Philologie* (1896) and his *Wörterbuch*, which together constitute the first and only (still today) systematic codification of the language and thus an impressive basis for interpretation. The final achievement of this first phase was also outstanding, namely the French translation by Jacques Duchesne-Guillemin (1948), the embodiment of the state of the art. Duchesne-Guillemin, using good common sense and excellent judgment, drew upon the various hypotheses concerning the problems in each particular passage and contributed himself a number of happy solutions. His translation is clear, transparently readable, and it even enables one to follow the movement of the thought through several strophes.

The surface meaning of the text, however, was by necessity sufficiently vague and capable of being manipulated to allow such divergent interpretations as the "fire teaching" of Johannes Hertel, the shamanism and ecstasy of Henrik S. Nyberg, the high politics of the court of Ernst Herzfeld, and the trifunctional ideology of Georges Dumézil. In fact, under the unanimous facade there was doubt, uncertainty, and suspicion. On one hand, Antoine Meillet wrote: "Although there remain several obscure passages, we can say that the general meaning of the *Gāθās* is known and that there is now consensus among the scholars who study them."[7] On the other hand, however, statements by other scholars expressed crudely a reality that was not, or only little or poorly, reflected in the finished products they handed in for publication. Thus Nyberg wrote: "whoever has dealt with these texts has resigned himself to translate differently in the morning from what he did the night before." And Kaj Barr: "The more I study the *Gāθās*, the less I understand them." The consensus over the surface meaning of the *Gāθās* was in fact nothing but a conventional agreement of last resort.

Bernfried Schlerath, in an extremely illuminating article published in 1962, discussed the problem and the history of studies. Schlerath underscored strongly Bartholomae's responsibility and contrasted Bartholomae's eminence as a grammarian with his dry formalism in analyzing living texts, where he exhibited a complete lack of feeling for

---

7   Meillet, 1925, p. 13.

what was likely. I do not subscribe to this judgment. Rather I believe it was Bartholomae's grammar that was still rudimentary. Do not understand me wrong. I am not questioning Bartholomae's work as a grammarian. It was a giant achievement, of high quality, which at the beginning of the century hoisted Avestan philology onto the level of the other principal Indo-European philologies. He did very well all one could do in 1904. The problem is that since then, for over fifty years, philology stagnated. This happened for various reasons, but mainly because of the illusions created by the Andreas theory and the subsequent disenchantment when that theory was refuted.

Twice it happened that, in the same year, Avestan studies were caught up in a paradox, where the past and the future collided head on. In 1902 Bartholomae presented the proofs of his *Wörterbuch* at the Orientalist conference in Hamburg on the very day that Andreas revealed his theory for the first time. fifty years later, in 1952, Duchesne-Guillemin's *Gāθā* translation appeared to receive the approval of Walter B. Henning, whose wife translated the French translation into English, at the exact moment when the first articles by Humbach appeared in the *Münchener Studien zur Sprachwissenschaft*, paving the way to the great break in Gathic studies, which was to be completed in 1959 with his *Die Gathas des Zarathustra*. Schlerath justly noted that this work marked an emancipation from Bartholomae.[8] Early on, Humbach's work was underestimated, however. It is plagued, it is true, by several striking faults. It is easy to joke that Humbach's German is more difficult than Zarathustra's Avestan and that the paraphrase sometimes has no connection to the text it is supposed to paraphrase. But that is unimportant. What is serious is Humbach's occasional lack of consistency. The reason is that his work was premature, as Duchesne-Guillemin clearly saw as soon as it became possible to see it.[9] As a student of Karl Hoffmann, Humbach worked in a perspective and employing methods that were still not full-borne and the theory of which had not yet been worked out. For instance, he applied to the injunctives the premises of Hoffmann's analysis, which itself was not to appear until in 1967. Thus he denied them the function of future tense, which had been favored by his predecessors, but then interpreted them almost exclusively as

---

8   Schlerath, 1962, p. 576.
9   Duchesne-Guillemin, 1974, p. 73.

past tense, ignoring the timelessness of these forms, which was to be Hoffmann's conclusion. Humbach also rejected explicitly the Andreas theory, practicing rigorous text criticism on the basis of Geldner's *Prolegomena*, which did not, however, prevent him from admitting four cases of false vocalization. A single one had been enough to open the doors to an Arsacid archetype!

Humbach also showed such a lack of concern for the meaning of the text that he gives his approval to serious contradictions. I shall mention two striking examples.

1. By the way he analyzed the injunctive, Humbach limited to a considerable extent references to the future and by excluding by the strictest etymological method the meaning of "retribution" in the sense of "retribution after death" for five or six words previously thought to have this meaning, he reduced the role of eschatology to the point that his translation contains nothing but a few curses for afterlife. At the end of his introduction, however, he thinks nothing of answering the question of what was the mainstay of the doctrine with "the eschatology."

2. In strophe Y.28.8 the speaker says clearly "Zarathustra and we." All the commentators put this passage, and this passage only, in quotation marks, imagining a congregation responding to the speaker. Otherwise, of course, one would have to admit that Zarathustra is not the regular speaker in the *Gāθās*. Humbach refused to resort to such a deplorable expedient, but silently. He does not point out the lack of consistency, and the very title of his book shows clearly that he considered Zarathustra to be the author and the speaker of the *Gāθās*.

These few points of criticism should not blind us to the fact that Humbach's work rendered that of all his predecessors obsolete. I therefore consider the practice exemplified recently in Philip Kreyenbroek's book about Sraoša somewhat perverse, where he lists all the translations of the Gathic strophes where *saraoša-* occurs, without discussing their respective merits and thus granting equal authority to all. But by such a procedure he denies that science itself obeys the laws of history. In the case of the *Gāθās*, one should give critical preference to Humbach's translation, which represents the most advanced stage of our present knowledge. Humbach radically brought the Gathic grammar up to date by applying all the progress achieved in the field of Vedic grammar. Thus his undertaking is characterized by a return to the pure and hard method of comparison with the Vedas, which had not been practiced since the early works of Geldner and Bartholomae between 1870 and 1880. The fruitfulness of this method is at the same time the clear proof that it is legitimate and appropriate for the study of the Old Avesta. The discipline required for the study of these texts is certainly not Indology, nor is it just Iranology, but exactly this kind of Indo-Iranology that I spoke of earlier. The Vedic and the Old Avestan texts agree not only in grammar but also in style. Humbach systematically quoted the parallel phrases in the Rigveda, which often furnish the key to a verse. On average, every other verse has a Rigvedic parallel. While the religious doctrine may have been something new (and there are still nuances to be worked out), the language, the rhetoric, the concepts that nourish images and metaphors were surprisingly conservative and similar to those practiced by the Vedic *ṛsis*. It is hardly an exaggeration to say the Old Avesta is the eleventh *maṇḍala* of the Rigveda, only written in a slightly different dialect.

With Humbach the Gathic paradox changed shape. The meaning of the text now became just as obscure or nonsensical as the grammatical doctrine it was based upon became solid and coherent. Humbach exploded the agreement on the surface meaning, but that negative effect also seemed to be the only result of his contribution. Thus Schlerath, taking a dig at Humbach, was able to write that the Zarathustra of certain grammarians was no more than a speaker of stupidities.[10] Humbach freed the exegesis of the *Gāθās* from Bartholomae for good, but his work left the impression of something unfulfilled. Others therefore took up the task.

So where are we today? My opinion will be biased, as I am one of those who considered it important to continue on the road staked out by Humbach. But for the same reason, perhaps my opinion, although biased, may be of some interest. Let me say that Humbach gave us an appropriate morphology of Old Avestan, but he left the syntax fallow. Stanley Insler first, then Eric Pirart and myself, attempted to remedy this situation. Others will have to judge whether we have succeeded or not. It is clear, however, that our combined efforts have not resolved the problem of the *Gāθās*. Will it be resolved one day? I am relatively optimistic. If we know the language of a text sufficiently well the text can not remain for ever incomprehensible, that is, unless it is deliberately hermetic. I for one, however, differently

---

[10] In Lommel, 1971, p. 10.

from others, do not believe it is. It seems to me that the difficulty of the text is its semantics, which is the diagnosis Schlerath gave it in 1962. We have today a good morphology and, for the sake of argument at least, a good syntax. With these tools we can define the place of the words and should be able, over the next years, to define their meaning.

The great merit of Humbach's work is to have demonstrated that in reality there is no paradox nor any mystery of the *Gāθās*. We did not know the language as well as we thought, and the contents were not really what we supposed they were. The *Gāθās* are a text like any other text. Their grammar must be patiently perfected, and their meaning must be sought by means of just this grammar, without excessive concern for whatever Zarathustra is supposed to have said.

LECTURE II. THE GODS

THROUGHOUT THE HISTORY of the religion, Ahura Mazdā enjoyed an incomparable prestige in the Mazdean pantheon, and his name is mentioned everywhere in the texts. He is by no means the only divine person of the religious universe, however. In the Old Avesta one finds at his sides not the gods of the Indo-Iranian pantheon, either in its Vedic or Young Avestan version, but a group of divine beings one traditionally calls the six Aməša Spəntas, approximately, "beneficent immortals." This group, which appears to constitute one of the most markedly original features of the Old Avestan Mazdaism, poses a specific but difficult question. It is significant that Western learning is reluctant to speak about "gods" to denote the beings it consists of, preferring "entity" (Germ. "Wesenheit") or simply using for the sake of convenience the Avestan terms *aməša spənta*. There are two, more or less good, reasons for not granting these "entities" complete divine status. The names of the three most important ones is neuter, and each of them is an abstract noun which most often functions as such and is only sporadically, or rarely, personified.

The six entities as listed explicitly in the Young Avesta are in the order of frequency in the Old Avesta: Aša, Vohu Manah, Xšaθra, Ārmaiti, Aməratāt, and Hauruuatāt. French philologists translate Aša as "order" or "justice," the German ones as "truth." The common denominator of these quite differing interpretations is the etymological meaning of the word, which is "ordered structure." Vohu Manah is "good thought" (that is, from a ritual point of view). Xšaθra signifies "power," but in the *Gāθās* at least it is not a political power. Humbach defines it as "the magical power (*Potenz*) by which the priest makes the deity favorable to him." Ārmaiti is "good spiritual disposition" (that is, from a ritual point of view), the thought which takes into consideration in appropriate manner, without rejecting as too trifling or neglecting anything. Hauruuatāt and Aməratāt are, respectively, "wholeness of the body" and "immortality."

The structure and meaning of this group have been interpreted in three different ways throughout the history of studies. To make the following exposition clearer, let me recall them briefly and schematically.

The oldest interpretation reproduces in the main the analysis of the Pahlavi treatises of the 9th-10th centuries of our era, namely the *Bundahišn* and the *Dēnkard.* Here, each entity personifies and patrons a natural element: Aṣa the fire, Vohu Manah the cow, Xšaθra the metals, Ārmaiti the earth, Hauruuatāt the waters, and Amərətāt the plants. This hypothesis, which we shall refer to as the "element hypothesis," is still defended with rich nuances which I do not have the time to review and is still today the hypothesis accepted by a majority of scholars. It appeared at the beginning of studies when it was stated with great decisiveness by Herman Lommel in his *Religion Zarathustras* (1930), and it has today the honors of the broad synthesis of Mary Boyce, *History of Zoroastrianism* (vol. 1, 1975), which is presently regarded as the authority on the matter.

In 1945, Georges Dumézil, in his *Naissance d'Archanges*, endeavored to show that the function of the group of entities was to reproduce the tripartite organization of the divine world, the frames of which, according to Dumézil, had been compromised by the decay of the traditional pantheon but which had remained too strong an ideological scheme to be abandoned completely. Aṣa and Vohu Manah incarnated the magico-religious sovereignty, the former in its Varuṇian aspect, the latter in its Mitrian aspect. Xšaθra incorporated the warrior function, and Hauruuatāt and Amərətāt, frequently coupled grammatically in a *dvandva*, constituted the twin couple in charge of fecundity. Dumézil found no place for Ārmaiti in 1945, but later she was assigned an acceptable position, when Stig Wikander interpreted the figure of Draupadī within the trifunctional configuration of the heroes of the *Mahābhārata* and suggested that she was the feminine entity that transcends the functions and incorporates them one after the other. Note that Dumézil does not deny the element hypothesis. He only contests its primary character, seeing in it the effect of the trifunctional ideology. It seems logical that the representatives of fecundity should patron the earthly powers of life, water, and plants, and that Xšaθra should personify the metal, of which weapons are made. The scheme is less satisfactory for the first function. We may admit that Aṣa, being substituted for Varuṇa, should be the patron of the fire, because fire constitutes the "prime substance" of reality, but there is nothing in the Avesta that proves that this is how the role of fire in the universe was conceived. The scholarly gymnastics become very contorted when one attempts to explain how and why the Mitrian sovereign's vocation is to protect the cow.

finally, in 1982, Johanna Narten, in her *Die Aməṣa Spəṇtas im Avesta*, reexamined the facts of the problem from top to bottom applying rigorously, by reaction to the speculative tendencies of her predecessors, the method consisting of accepting only the textual facts and evaluating precisely the degree of probability of each of them. Her examination resulted first in two observations, which makes it possible to define the problem more exactly.

1.   The title of *aməša spənta* in fact is Young Avestan. Although the two words are mentioned together twice in the *Yasna Haptaŋhāiti*, it is an anachronism, even if it seems convenient, to use the title for the Old Avestan entities. In the *Gāθās*, the entities are called *ahura*s, with the same title bestowed on them as on Mazdā.

2.   In the Young Avesta it is said explicitly that the Aməša Spəntas are seven, but the list never contains more than six names. There is no way one may recruit Sraoša or Spənta Maniiu. The missing Aməša Spənta is the first of the list, who is always mentioned separately, Ahura Mazdā himself.

Next, Narten arrives at an extremely important conclusion: the Old Avestan entities are not, either in the *Gāθās* or the *Yasna Haptaŋhāiti*, represented by the group of six "beneficent immortals," which was not constituted until in the Young Avesta. Instead they form an open list. They can not be identified or enumerated other than by studying in minute detail and with great circumspection their scattered features of personification. After her investigation, Narten gives a detailed catalogue of the entities in the *Gāθās* (pp. 53-54): Aša, Vohu Manah, and Ārmaiti, as well as ("auch") Spənta Maniiu and Xšaθra, occasionally ("gelegentlich") Səraoša and Aši, in rudiments ("in Ansätzen") Hauruuatāt and Aməratāt, perhaps ("vielleicht") Daēnā. Thus Narten removes every support for the interpretation at the archaic period of a system of the entities within the framework of the group of six "beneficent immortals." Clearly, if the list is not closed, there is no structure. The last chapters of the book are devoted to refuting the element hypothesis. She shows that in the Old Avesta the entities are never set in logical relation with the elements. The only feature one might mention is the repeated statement (Y.34.4, 43.4) that the ritual fire owes its *aogah* "authority" to Aša, but it would be hazardous to conclude that Aša is primarily the divine patron of the cosmic element fire. In contrast, Narten mentions the tripartite hypothesis only briefly (p. 104 n. 12). This theory can only be accepted if, throughout the Mazdean tradition, neither the list of entities nor its hierarchy ever varied. Clearly, both conditions are swept away by her analysis. The trifunctional analysis is excluded as soon as there is no structured list. I would like to add for my own part that two details seem to refute Dumézil's analysis:

1. Much complacency is needed in order to attribute the warrior function to any Old Avestan entity, and Xšaθra is not a more obvious candidate that any of the others. We must admit that in the entire Old Avesta there is total silence regarding the warrior. That does not mean, however, that there exists a Gathic pacifism, as has sometimes been stated. There is no indication that the speaker condemns the brutality of his enemies any more than he exalts the pacifism of his own community. We can only note the fact that warrior activities are simply absent from the Old Avestan horizon. Our information is too limited for us to know whether we are dealing with a value judgment or whether war is outside the concerns of the liturgical and literary genre.

2. Dumézil recognized the Varuṇa-type sovereign in Aṣa and the Mitra-type sovereign in Vohu Manah essentially on the basis of an obsolete interpretation of Y.29. It used to be argued that the entity who speaks in strophe 8 to give the cow a patron is Vohu Manah, because his name figures in the preceding strophe in the instrumental and the instrumental was supposed to be able to be used as a vocative. Humbach, however, showed conclusively that this hypothesis of the nominative and vocative functions of the instrumental was illusory. The fact that the name of Vohu Manah is in the instrumental in a question is, on the contrary, an undeniable sign that the question is not addressed to him.

On the whole, we can say that both the element hypothesis and the tripartite hypothesis are refuted by their being gratuitous. To take the most striking example, Aṣa is mentioned 151 times in the *Gāθās*. In at least 145 of these passages, the passages in question are not made more comprehensible if one keeps in mind that Aṣa actually stands for either the element fire or the Varuṇa-type sovereign. And even in the half a dozen strophes which seem to bear up either of the two hypotheses, we have to reckon with illusion and uncertainty. The system of entities must obey another logic.

We have to come back to the question of the instrumental, for if Dumézil was victim of the ideas one had of its usage, so, to a certain extent, was Johanna Narten. The earliest interpreters of the *Gāθās*—Geldner, Caland, and Bartholomae—had already been struck by the statistical fact that the name of Mazdā is never attested in the instrumental, while the three entities of neuter gender, Aša, Vohu Manah, and Xšaθra, are most often in that case. Therefore, there seemed to be a direct relationship between the system of the entities and the inordinately frequent use of the instrumental, and one was easily tempted to try to explain this situation by assuming that this grammatical peculiarity was suited to a conceptual innovation. According to an old hypothesis that Eduard Schwijzer had systematized in 1929, the instrumental could be substituted for the nominative and vocative of transitive verbs. It was possible to believe that the extension of this usage was due to the emergence of a certain form of monotheism. According to an interpretation that reached its high point with Maria Wilkins Smith and which profoundly influenced Duchesne-Guillemin's translation, the instrumental did not really represent the subject of the verb as such or the person invoked, but the particular aspect in which this person was supposed to be acting at the moment. When Ahura Mazdā performs an action and the verb that expresses this action is accompanied by the instrumental of the names of Aša, Vohu Manah, or Xšaθra, that meant that Ahura Mazdā acted as Aša, Vohu Manah, or Xšaθra. The entities were therefore nothing but punctual modes of the activity of Ahura Mazdā, his aspects, his hypostases. This interpretation is an example of the postulate and, frankly, of the incurable tendency of Western scholarship to make its own Mazdean theology. In my opinion, it is possible to discuss the matter in a relaxed fashion and to explain with a high degree of probability and without exception all the Old Avestan instrumentals without leaving the framework established by Delbrück's *Altindische Syntax*. Humbach made a brave but imperfect effort. While rejecting the substitution of the instrumental for the nominative and vocative, he increased the category of the comitative instrumental boundlessly. The comitative, however, can only be used with persons. Humbach also analyzed some instrumentals as adnominal, in spite of the fact that the only adnominal case of the ancient Indo-Iranian declension is the genitive, with a few well-defined exceptions. Narten followed his lead to a certain extent, but remained too dependent upon the old idea of the instrumental. She admitted comitative functions too generously and even made it a certain criterion of personification. It is not possible, however, to conclude from Y.43.6 *θβā maniiū ... jasō* that the notion of *spəṇta- maniiu-* is personified, as the passage does not necessarily mean "you come together with your *maniiu*" but more probably "you come because of [*grâce à*] *or* on account of [*en raison de*] your *maniiu*." The comitative function is never more than one possibility among others, and by keeping it as a criterion of personification, from a methodological point of view, one is bound to be caught up in a vicious circle of assuming that, because a noun designating a person in the instrumental regularly matches the comitative function, any instrumental presumed to be comitative must be a noun designating a person. It is preferable to leave the instrumental out of the discussion altogether, retaining only the vocative, the assignment of a divine title, and a family metaphor (e.g., "son of") as signs of personification. In this way one may count six entities: Aṣa, Vohu Manah, Ārmaiti, Xšaθra, Ādā, and Daēnā, of which the last three are included on the basis of a single passage each; *xšaθra* is found coordinated with Ahura Mazdā, Aṣa, Vohu Manah, and Ārmaiti in an expression that functions as a vocative (Y.33.11); *ādā-* is personified both by the use of the vocative and the assignment of the title *vohu-*, which means both "good" and "divine" (Y.49.1); *daēnā-* is among the *haṇt*s "those who are (always)" (Y.44.10). It is preferable not to take them too seriously into account, because, as we shall see, their personification has other means of expression and because its wholly exceptional character coincides with the absence of any family metaphor. It seems, therefore, that the family metaphor is the real touchstone. Three frequent and prestigious entities are presented in the *Gāθās* as the children of Ahura Mazdā: Aṣa, Vohu Manah, and Ārmaiti. There is a subtle lack of symmetry between the two entities of neuter gender, who are both inactive (they rarely function as subject and never of "to be"), and the feminine entity, more rarely mentioned, but in all cases personified, and who can be, like Ahura Mazdā, the subject of a verb of action.

Nevertheless, the actual list of entities is not closed with those three. They form a kind of hard core, around which there gravitate virtual or less important entities, which we can classify in three categories:

1. The following I would propose to recognize and define as "entities by association": the concepts of *aṣi-* "share," *hauruuatāt-* "integrity of the body," *amaratāt-* "immortality," *utaiiūiti-* "youthfulness," and *tauuīṣī-* "robustness." None of these are personified by the criteria we have set up, but they are systematically dragged along in the wake of Ārmaiti, with whom they share the grammatical gender. This is the concession I believe

we have to make to the comitative instrumental. The personification of
Ārmaiti is permanent, but also contagious.

2. As Humbach strongly underlined, the Old Avestan rhetoric has a strong
    propensity for synecdoche and metonomy. In principle, we are dealing
    with pure figures of style, but they have also been capable of giving birth
    to, or at any rate they will give birth to, deified incarnations of various
    aspects of human piety. The two great entities Vohu Manah and Ārmaiti
    are partly a product of synecdoche, but we shall see that this is not enough
    to account for their divine status. It is possible that the style figure has
    already proceeded to the status of conceptual reality with *daēnā-*, who is
    presented as a divinity in Y.44.10, but this insubstantial part of man, which
    ensures the connection between the being and its permanence in the next
    world, was predisposed for a certain independence. On the other hand, it
    is certain that the synecdoche was responsible for adding the entities
    Spəṇta Maniiu and Sraoša to the list of Aməša Spəṇtas in the Young
    Avesta.

3. finally, we have the ritual allegories, comparable to the Vedic *tisró devíḥ*
    and represented by *xšaθra-* "ritual power over the gods" and *ādā-* "deposi-
    tory for the offering." Like the latter, *īžā-* "invigoration" and *āzūiti-*
    "libation" were elevated to the rank of entity in the *Yasna Haptaŋhāiti*, as
    were their Vedic equivalents *íḍā-* and *ā́huti-*.

Let me summarize my position on the question of the entities by
distinguishing between two kinds of facts. In one way the list is closed. A
triad of entities subordinated to Ahura Mazdā is accorded divine rank.
Those are the ones Narten cites unreservedly. Beside this group, however,
which indeed constitutes the originality of the doctrine, we find an open list
of personified abstractions with no fixed number. These are the effect of
the capacity of Old Avestan rhetoric to "produce" entities, by synecdoche or
by allegory. The Aməša Spəṇtas of the Young Avesta were constituted by
including the entire triad plus select members of the second group.

In his review of Narten's book, Prods O. Skjærvø wrote, with a certain
wistfulness, that the best service the author could have rendered to the
question of the Aməša Spəṇtas would have been to publish her edition of
the *Yasna Haptaŋhāiti*. This is today a *fait accompli*, and it is quite clear
that the *Yasna Haptaŋhāiti* contains essential evidence for understanding the
entities. It is this text which contains for the first time the expression
aməša- spəṇta-, even though Narten makes little of its importance. Let us

look at this point more closely, and first of all let us get an idea of the structure of the *Yasna Haptaŋhāiti*.

After two chapters of introduction, the first devoted to the ritual act (*šiiaoθana-*) and the second to the consecration of the fire, we arrive at the center of the text, the actual Yasna, that is, a litany in *yazamaidē* "we sacrifice":

Yasna 37
1. *iθā āṯ yazamaidē ahurəm mazdąm yə gąmcā ašəmcā dāṯ apascā dāṯ uruuaråscā vaŋ^hīš raocåscā dāṯ būmīmcā vīspācā vohū*
2. *ahiiā xšaθrācā mazānācā hauuapaŋhāišcā tōm aṯ yasnanąm pauruuatātā yazamaidē yōi gōuš hacā šiieiṇtī*
3. *tōm aṯ āhūriiā nāmōnī mazdā varā spəṇtō.təmā yazamaidē tōm ahmākāiš azdəbīšcā uštānāišcā yazamaidē tōm ašāunąm frauuašīš narąmcā nāirinąmcā yazamaidē*
4. *ašəm aṯ vahištəm yazamaidē hiiaṯ sraēštəm hiiaṯ spəṇtəm aməšəm hiiaṯ raocōŋhuuaṯ hiiaṯ vīspā vohū*
5. *vohucā manō yazamaidē vohucā xšaθrəm vaŋ^hīmcā daēnąm vaŋ^hīmcā fsəratūm vaŋ^hīmcā ārmaitīm*

Yasna 38
1. *imąm āaṯ ząm gənābīš haθrā yazamaidē yā nå baraitī yåscā tōi gənå ahura.mazdā ašāṯ hacā vairiiå tå yazamaidē*
2. *īžå yaoštaiiō fəraštaiiō ārmataiiō vaŋ^hīm ābīš ašīm vaŋ^hīm īšəm vaŋ^hīm āzūitīm vaŋ^hīm frasastīm vaŋ^hīm parōṇdīm yazamaidē*
3. *apō aṯ yazamaidē maēkaiṇtīšcā həbuuaiṇtīšcā frauuazaŋhō ahurānīš ahurahiiā huuapaŋhō hupərəθβåscā vå huuō.ẏžaθåscā hūšnāθråscā ubōibiiā ahubiiā cagəmā*
4. *ūitī yā vō vaŋ^hīš ahurō mazdå nāmąn dadāṯ vaŋhudå hiiaṯ vå dadāṯ tāiš vå yazamaidē tāiš friiąnmahī tāiš nəmaxiiāmahī tāiš išūidiiāmahī*
5. *apascā vå azīšcā vå mātərąšcā vå agəniiå drigudāiiaŋhō vīspō.paitīš āuuaocāmā vahištå sraēštå auuā vō vaŋ^hīš rātōiš darəgō.bāzāuš nāšū paitī viiādå paitī.sōṇdå mātarō jītaiiō*

Yasna 39
1. *iθā āṯ yazamaidē gōuš uruuānəmcā tašānəmcā ahmākōŋg āaṯ urunō pasukanąmcā yōi nå jījišəṇtī yaēibiiascā tōi ā yaēcā aēibiiō ā aŋhən*
2. *daitikanąmcā aidiiūnąm hiiaṯ urunō yazamaidē ašāunąm āaṯ urunō yazamaidē kudō.zātanąmcīṯ narąmcā nāirinąmcā yaēšąm vahehīš daēnå vanaiṇtī vā vōŋghən vā vaonarə vā*
3. *āaṯ iθā yazamaidē vaŋhūšcā īṯ vaŋ^hīšcā īṯ spəṇtōŋg aməšōŋg yauuaējiiō yauuaēsuuō yōi vaŋhōuš ā manaŋhō šiieiṇtī yåscā uitī*

4. *yaθā tū ī ahura.mazdā mə̄nghācā vaocascā dåscā varəšcā yā vohū aθā tōi dadəmahī aθā cīšmahī aθā θβā āiš yazamaidē aθā nəmax̌iiāmahī aθā išūidiiāmahī θβā mazdā ahurā*

5. *vaŋhə̄uš xᵛaētə̄uš xᵛaētātā vaŋhə̄uš ašahiiā θβā pairijasāmaidē vaŋhuiiå fsəratuuō vaŋhuiiå ārmatōiš*

Translation

Yasna 37

1. Thus we offer sacrifice to Ahura Mazdā who has put in their proper place the cow and Aṣa, put in their proper place the waters and the good plants, put in their proper place the heavenly lights, the earth, and all good things (in between),

2. thanks to the influence upon him, by his greatness and his expertise. We offer him sacrifice with the first choice of sacrifices, who ... the cow.

3. Adoring Ahura, we offer him the sacrifice (speaking his) names "Mazdā," "beloved," "very beneficent." We offer him the sacrifice with our bones and our life spirits. We offer him the sacrifice with our preferences of partisans of Aṣa, men and women.

4. We offer the sacrifice to the very good Aṣa, who is very beautiful, who is an Aməṣa Spəṇta, who is in charge of the (celestial) lights, who is in charge of all good things (in between).

5. We offer the sacrifice to Vohu Manah, the good Xšaθra, to the good Daēnā, to the good Fsəratū, and to the good Ārmaiti.

Yasna 38

1. We offer the sacrifice to the firm earth here at the same time as to the goddesses; we offer the sacrifice to the firm earth, which carries us, and to the goddesses, your daughters, worthy of being elected, o Ahura Mazdā,

2. women such as Īžā, Yaošti, Fərašti, Ārmaiti; as to these we also offer the sacrifice to the good Aṣi, to the good Īš, to the good Āzūiti, to the good Frasasti, to the good Parə̄ṇdi.

3. We offer the sacrifice to the waters, as well as to those that ... as to those that ... Daughters and wives of the Ahura, (you) who drive forth and are endowed with expertise, we offer you a gift, because, for the two states you are easy to cross, you .... and you offer good baths.

4. We offer you the sacrifice, we propitiate you, we render you homage, we bring you vigor pronouncing the names that Ahura Mazdā gives you when he makes you render all things good.

5. We say of you, waters, of you, milch cows, of you, mothers, that you are exuberant, that you nourish those who have need, that you water everyone, that you are good and very beautiful.

Yasna 39

1.   Thus we offer the sacrifice to the *uruuan* of the cow and to Gə̄uš Tašan, to our *uruuan*s and to those of the domestic animals which try to gain our favor, the favor of the men who dispose over them and the favor of the men they dispose over,

2.   and also the sacrifice to the *uruuan* of the wild beasts, inasmuch as they are harmless. We offer the sacrifice to the *uruuan* of the followers of Aṣa, men and women, whose very good *daēnā*s are winning, will win, or have won.

3.   Thus we offer the sacrifice to the good male and female Aməṣa Spəṇtas, who live for ever and prosper for ever, who have their quarters near the cow.

4.   The good (thought) as you have thought it, the good (word) as you have spoken it, the good (ritual institution) as you have founded it, the good (deed) as you have done it, we perform them on you, we address them to you, and through them we offer you the sacrifice, we render you homage, and we bring you vigor, o Ahura Mazdā.

5.   We serve you by manifesting our specific belonging to the good family of the good Aṣa, of the good Fsəratū, and the good Ārmaiti.

Paragraphs Y.37.1-39.4, in which *yazamaide* governs the noun Ahura Mazdā, are an echo of closure. The expression *aməṣə̄ṇg spəṇtə̄ṇg* in Y.39.3 can not be an additional item to the list of the concepts worthy of receiving the *yasna*. That is not possible as long as the title *aməṣa spəṇta* has been explicitly applied to Aṣa, the first entity directly after Ahura Mazdā to be made the object of a *yazamaide*, and the names of the list cover in part those of the entities and of the seven "beneficent immortals" of the Young Avesta. Y.39.3 is necessarily a recapitulation. This is all the more evident as *iθā* echoes Y.37.1 and *aməṣə̄ṇg spəṇtə̄ṇg* echoes Y.37.4, so that it appears that the closing phase of the ensemble Y.37-39 starts with Y.39.3. Narten interprets this phrase ambiguously. She defines it as a "comprehensive formulation" (*umfassende Formulierung*), but only after having limited the scope of this resume:

"With this expression [*aməṣa spəṇta*] reference is therefore again made to entities of the kind to which belong those mentioned in chapter 37, among them *aṣa*, one of whose epithets is *aməṣa-spəṇta-*, but also *īžā-*, *yaošti-*, etc. (39.2), even though these, precisely in connection with *zam-* (38.1), clearly show themselves to be a separate group. It is obvious from the names as such that they nevertheless belong with the entities mentioned in chapter 37 and also from the twice repeated mention of *ārmaiti-* (37.5; 38.2), by which the two groups are connected. One is therefore led to assume that this last *yazamaidē* sentence was intended as a general (*allgemeingültige*) formulation comprising all the entities of this kind without naming any of them."

If we assign a recapitulating function to Y.39.3—which seems to be the only reasonable thing to do—then we also have to draw the conclusion, unreservedly, that the term *aməša spəṇta* is applied to all the concepts without exception whose names have been the object of *yazamaidē*. There is no textual or objective reason for making a selection. Nothing allows us to exclude from the rank of the Haptahatic Aməša Spəṇtas the earth and the waters. As for Gəuš Tašan and the various *uruuans*, I confess I am at a loss. The question is connected with that of the use of *iθā* "thus," which is rarely found and therefore not well understood. The presence of this adverb in Y.37.1 and Y.39.3 is understandable. Here it introduces the initial sentence (Y.37.1) and by echo the first of the concluding sentences (Y.39.3), referring back to the first two chapters. "Thus" is an economical way of saying "by the triad of thought, word, deed (Y.35) and by placing oneself next to the sacred fire (Y.36)." On the other hand, I do not understand the reason for its use at the beginning of Y.39.1. I can think of two hypotheses. Either the situation expressed by *iθā* referred to all the *yazamaidē*, and the litany therefore became too long to sustain the *sous-entendu*, or the sentence means Gəuš Tašan and the various *uruuans* will receive sacrifice "thus," that is, like the others, which implies that they are not of the same category. The question remains, therefore, whether they belong to the group of Aməša Spəṇtas or not.

We should note that the first sentence (Y.37.1) justifies the cult of Ahura Mazdā by the grandiose character of his founding action, which is expressed by the verb *dā* governing the accusative alone, although there are several coordinated objects, forming a contrasting pair in the first two groups (the Cow and Aša, the waters and the plants), a triad in the third group. This usage of *dā* corresponds to the meaning of putting something in its proper place. What is the meaning of the triad? The opposition between *raocah-*, literally "light," and *būmi-* "terrestrial space" shows that *raocah-* is the Haptahatic word used to designate the sky, corresponding to Gathic *nabah-*, literally "cloud." My interpretation of *vīspāca vohū* as "all good things (in the intermediary space)" is suggested both by its place in the triad and explicitly by Yt.13.153 *imąmca ząm ... aomca asmanəm ... tāca vohū ... yā antarəstā* "this earth and that sky and those good things that are in between" (the final long *ū* of *vohū* and *ā* of *antarəstā* suggest that this is an old gloss). We are therefore dealing with the three spaces: celestial, terrestrial, and atmospheric.

The epithets *raocōŋhuuat̰* and *vīspā.vohū* in Y.37.4 applied to Aša evidently refer to the *raocåscā ... vīspāca vohū* of Ahura Mazdā's third establishment. They point out that Aša belongs to the celestial and intermediary space. In this way a bond is established between those "put in their place" by Ahura Mazdā and the entities which receive the *yasna*, a bond which gives us the key to the analysis of the former and the structure of the group formed by the latter. The elements Ahura Mazdā has put in their place are distributed over two pairs and one triad in contrast.: 1 the cow and Aša, 2. the waters and the plants, 3. the sky, the earth, and the intermediary space. The first pair and the triad overlap in part chiastically. Aša, the great celestial and atmospheric entity, as is made explicit in Y.37.4, corresponds to *raocåscā ... vīspāca vohū*, and the cow, as the ultimate living being, corresponds to *būmīmcā*. The second pair expresses a secondary opposition subdividing the sphere represented by the earth and by the cow. It distinguishes in the terrestrial space (*būmi-*) two sub-elements that constitute the food of the cow: the waters and the plants, which the waters make sprout from the solid earth.

The list of entities contained in Y.37.4-39.2 is thus essentially composed of abstractions associated with the spheres that constitute the universe and of some of these very spheres. Its structure is dictated by the primary opposition between the sky, the atmosphere, and the earth and the secondary opposition, grafted onto the "earth," between the solid earth and the water. Thus we have:

1.   the celestial and atmospheric entities (Y.37.4, 5): Aša, Vohu Manah, Xšaθra, Daēnā, Fsəratū, and Ārmaiti;

2.   the terrestrial entities (Y.38): Zam, Īžā, Yaošti, Fərašti, Ārmaiti, Aši, Īš, Āzūiti, Frasasti, Parəndi, Āp. Ārmaiti is special, as it figures in both categories.

3. Gōuš Tašan and the undying principle (*uruuan*) of certain living beings:
the cow, the sacrificers ("we"), the domestic animals, the harmless wild
animals, and the men in the camp of Aša (Y.39.1-2). I already mentioned,
however, that we should take this last group with some reservation.

Groups 1 and 2 are visibly hierarchical. In the first Aša stands out
clearly. It is cited first, takes up by itself one of the two sentences, and is
entitled to a series of epithets. In the second group the natural elements
enjoy a certain predilection. It does seem that the associative instrumental
serves to subordinate the feminine entities considered as *gənā-* "divine
women" to the earth. The individual female deities are for their part
subordinated to the feminine entities. The waters, finally, are invoked by
themselves and with remarkable insistence (three long sentences!). We
should also note that Ahura Mazdā can not be ranked with the Haptahatic
Aməša Spəṇtas, as they represent what he has established, and the group is
strictly demarcated by the echo Y.37.4 *spəṇtəm aməšəm* — Y.39.3 *spəṇtåṅg
aməšåṅg*.

The entities to whom the title of Aməša Spəṇta is assigned in the *Yasna
Haptaŋhāiti* are partly the same ones that surround Ahura Mazdā in the
Gāθās. In both texts the group is headed by Aša, Vohu Manah, and
Ārmaiti, with the addition of Xšaθra and Daēnā. The apparent differences
are the following:

1. The *Gāθās* do not contain the title *aməša spəṇta*, and the title *ahura-*,
which appears to be used in its place, is not exclusively applied to the
entities. It is applied to Mazdā himself, of course, but also to the ritual fire
and Zaraθuštra, and, perhaps as a "lay" title, to the owner of cattle.

2. In contrast to the Gathic list, the Haptahatic list of entities is almost closed.
Only the plurals in Y.38.2 indicate that the entities mentioned may be
mere examples representing a larger group. The author of the *Yasna
Haptaŋhāiti* prefers to express himself by a list, which the author of the
Gāθās never does. It is therefore possible that in the *Yasna Haptaŋhāiti*
the list was in the process of being fixed.

3. In the *Gāθās* it is not certain that the solid earth and the waters belong to
the rank of entities. If they do, as Y.33.10 might seem to indicate, at least
they are not as important as the other entities. This would mean that the
doctrine of the *Yasna Haptaŋhāiti* was somewhat more naturalist.

4.   In the *Gāθās* it is Y.44.3-7 that bear witness to the association of the
     entities with the cosmic spheres. Aṣa and Vohu Manah are associated
     with all the three spaces together, and each of their invocations (Y.44.3bb'
     and 4cc') concludes and closes the passage devoted to the description of
     how they were established. Ārmaiti is mentioned only in connection with
     living beings (Y.44.6, 7). The role of the entities is defined more precisely
     than in the *Yasna Haptaŋhāiti*, where they are only said to be
     raocōŋhuuaṇt- and *vīspā.vohū-*. The birth of the cosmic order is clearly
     presented as a preliminary to the cosmology and the birth of the ritual
     Thought as its ultimate act before the organization of the living world.
     The activity of Ārmaiti—support for Aṣa, ritual authority over Ahura
     Mazdā, use of Vohu Manah—ensures for the man who practices it the
     enjoyment of the cow. We shall have to come back to this.

5.   The entities never receive explicitly the sacrificial homage defined by *yaz*.
     In the *Yasna Haptaŋhāiti* it is therefore more clearly asserted, on one hand,
     that the entities are subordinated to Ahura Mazdā, because they are
     presented as established by him, and, on the other hand, that they are
     divine, because they are offered *yasna*. They are therefore quite clearly
     completely divine, but also subordinate.

It must be firmly emphasized that we are in no position to tell whether
these differences are real or illusory. It may all be caused by a difference of
perspective between the two texts. Perhaps the *Gāθās* and the *Yasna
Haptaŋhāiti* had exactly the same doctrine of the entities but for various
reasons it was not expounded in the *Gāθās* as systematically and technically
as in the *Yasna Haptaŋhāiti*. Once this is said, we must realize that, if but a
single one of these differences were real, we would have to conclude that
the Haptahatic system is closer to that of the Young Avesta. Such an
affinity might mean that the *Yasna Haptaŋhāiti* is slightly more recent than
the *Gāθās*, belongs to a different school, or reflects a different religious
dialect. Whatever the relationship between the two Old Avestan documents
may be, the system of the entities in the Young Avesta owes much to that of
the *Yasna Haptaŋhāiti*, from which it evolved by means of three operations:

1.   Selection of the celestial-atmospheric entities of Y.37.

2.   The inclusion of Ahura Mazdā, resulting in the fact that the Aməṣa
     Spəṇtas of the Young Avesta number seven, as do the divinities that are
     the object of *yazamaidē* in Y.37.

3.   Substitution of Hauruuatāt and Amərətāt for Daēnā and Fsəratū. Not only are these entities specifically Gathic, they also incorporate certain forces of fecundity, and in analogy to those in chapter Y.38 they are associated with the terrestrial space. The list of the Aməša Spəntas in the Young Avesta thus appears as a compromise list between the two Old Avestan documents and representative of the three cosmic spaces. It is possible that this operation could also correspond to the institution of a trifunctional structure.

To sum up let me say that the Old Avestan entities can not be precisely counted. In this sense the list is open, although not quite as much as Narten proposed. In the *Gāθās*, a dominating triad (Aša, Vohu Manah, Ārmaiti) tends to form a subordinate pantheon, while in the *Yasna Haptaŋhāiti* we are very close to a stable and hierarchical list. In both texts, the entities are emanations of the ordering of the cosmos. Yet they do not result from the "element" analysis of the cosmos, but from the old Indo-Iranian idea of the three spaces.

LECTURE III. THE LITURGY

ALTHOUGH ONE STILL regularly hears the tune about the anti-ritualism of the *Gāθās*, after the works of Humbach and Narten, no one contests anymore the fact that the *Gāθās* and the *Yasna Haptaŋhāiti* are liturgical texts. The frequent use of demonstrative pronouns referring to persons and events here and now and the performative (coincidence) value of the present indicative show that they were composed to accompany the stages of a ceremony. No concrete detail of the ceremony itself has been transmitted to us, however.

The Old Avestan texts do not describe the various parts of the sacrifice, but are a commentary upon its spirit by addressing themselves directly to Ahura Mazdā and his entities. Thus, their function is to talk to the gods about the ritual. Because the imperfection of our knowledge and the allusive nature of the texts often prevent us from knowing what is going on, the Gathic ritual has not only been interpreted in contradictory ways, but has often been underestimated, and its existence even denied.

Let me begin my analysis with a detail that ought to lead us beyond the ritual to the very conception of the gods seen in the Old Avesta, as well as of the organization of the world and the role played by human piety. At the same time, this detail will show us how incomprehensible the text would remain were it not for the fact that it is constantly interweaving the same motifs, seen in the same perspective, so that by combining parallel passages, whether external ones, namely the Rigveda, or internal Old Avestan ones, we are finally allowed to unravel the thread of the words and the thought.

The twice-attested Old Avestan (Gathic) word *dāman-* was until recently identified with Rigvedic *dhā́man-* and YAv. *dāman-*, both of which are extremely common and play an important conceptual role. It is well known that the Rigvedic word means approximately "divine institution, establishment" and that the YAv. word denotes the personal shares that the two demiurges, Ahura Mazdā and Aŋra Maniiu, assigned to themselves in the organization of the world. In 1975, however, in his interpretation of the *Gāθās*, Stanley Insler pointed out a detail that had till then remained unnoticed and which calls for another etymology. The word *dāman-* is in

close or immediate proximity to a word derived from the root *hi-* "to tie,"
once *haēθa-* "a tie, bond," and once *hiθao-* "binder, he who ties," which can
not just be coincidence. The two passages are the following:

> Y.46.6 *drūjō huuō dāmąn haēθahiiā gāṯ*
> Y.48.7 *aṣ̌ā viiąm yehiiā hiθāuš nā spəṇtō / aṯ hōi dāmąn θβahmī ā dąm ahurā*

The syntactic structure is the same: *dāman-* is determined by the genitive
of a word signifying either "bond" or "binder" (*hōi* refers to *hiθāuš*), which
is itself determined by the genitive of the name of Aṣ̌a (*yehiiā* refers to *aṣa*)
or of the Druj (*drūjō*). We can only conclude, whatever the implications
may be for the YAv. word, that the Rigvedic equivalent of OAv. *dāman-* is
not *dhā́man-* < *dhā-* "to place, establish," but in fact *dā́man-* < *dā-* "to tie,
bind." This interpretation is unavoidable but poses a serious semantic
problem: if *dāman-* and *haēθa-* both mean something like "bond," they can
only be in a possessive relationship (X of Y) if they are not exact synonyms
but complementary terms. Insler's solution—"bonds of captivity"—rests
upon the unprovable conviction that *hi* "has already acquired the special
meaning 'capture' in the Gathas."[11] If we examine the Vedic material, we
see in fact that *dā* and *si* refer to different techniques: *dā* refers to the act of
attaching something to a fixed support, while *si* refers to a system of ropes
and knots, a net, which immobilizes by pulling something tightly toward
itself. I would therefore like to propose that *haēθa-* is the "rope, string" or
the "cord-work" and *dāman-* the fixture to which this "cord-work" is
attached, that is, the picket (prop, pole, rod). In this way the grammatical
relationship between the two is easily explained. There is the "picket" of
the "rope" used by the one who arranges the rope or bonds of Aṣ̌a or of the
Druj.

Insler did not realize the fecundity of his etymology of *dāman-*. If we
consider Y.34.10 *dąmīm ... hiθąm aṣahiiā* and Y.48.7 *aṣā ... yehiiā hiθāuš
... hōi dāmąm*, which clearly combine the same ingredients, it becomes clear
that *dāmi-* is not a gratuitous synonym of *dātar-*, but the agent noun
corresponding to *dāman-*, like *hiθao-* is the agent noun corresponding to
haēθa-. We have here he who plants the picket, the action needed before
the cord-work can be attached.

---

[11] [Insler, 1975, p. 147.]

We are now in a position to see what the image of the pickets and the cords is about. The act by which Ahura Mazdā (Y.34.10) or a pious man (Y.48.7) "binds" Aṣa can obviously not be a negative act. In this context, the function of the pickets and the rope can not be to restrain a prisoner, but clearly to lend coherence and solidity to a collection of items. The image is neither war-like nor pastoral, but architectural. The pickets and the cord-work of Aṣa are the elements of the metaphor that represents the act by which Ahura Mazdā put the universe in order as that of raising a tent. The Old Avesta expresses other features graphically, albeit more seldom: *dar-* "uphold" must be understood literally and concretely when applied to Aṣa (Y.31.7, 43.1, 46.3, 51.8), the "covering" (*viiā-*) that must be "firmly attached" (*dranj*) in Y.48.7, *dəbqz* and its derivative *dəbqzah-* refer to the lateral supports (Y.44.6, 47.6). Thus, the metaphor of the cosmic hut, the traces of which in the Indo-European domain were recently exhibited by Alain Christol, had its Iranian version as well.

What characterizes the Iranian motif, however, is its very special importance in the religious doctrine. The first indication of its importance, and the most general one, is the very frequency of the metaphor. Of the 240 Gathic strophes, about twenty contain it more or less complete, which is a lot! It is even more significant that the image of the raising of the tent is the only cosmogonic scheme retained in the *Avesta*: it is, in fact, the orthodox cosmogony of the Avestan Mazdaism, both Old Avestan and Young Avestan. The theory is expounded in strophes 3 to 7 of *hāiti* Y.44:

3. *taṭ θβā pərəsā arəš mōi vaocā ahurā*
    kasnā zq̇θā ptā aṣahiiā pouruiiō
    kasnā xᵛə̄ng strə̄mcā dāṭ aduuānəm
    kə̄ yā må uxšiieitī nərəfsaitī θβaṭ
    tācīṭ mazdā vasəmī aniiācā vīduiiē

4. *taṭ θβā pərəsā arəš mōi vaocā ahurā*
    kasnā dərətā zq̇mcā adə̄ nabåscā
    auuapastōiš kə̄ apō uruuaråscā
    kə̄ vātāi duuq̇nmaibiiascā yaogəṭ āsū
    kasnā vaŋhə̄uš mazdā dq̇miš manaŋhō

5. *taṭ θβā pərəsā arəš mōi vaocā ahurā*
    kə̄ huuāpå raocåscā dāṭ təmåscā

kə̄ huuāpå x^vafnəmcā dāt̰ zaēmācā
kə̄ yā ušå arəm.piθβā xšapācā
yå manaoθrīš cazdōŋhuuaṇtəm arəθahiiā

6.   *tat̰ θβā pərəsā arəš mōi vaocā ahurā*
yā frauuaxšiiā yezī tā aθā haiθiiā
ašəm šiiaoθanāiš dəbązaitī ārmaitiš
taibiiō xšaθrəm vohū cinas manaŋhā
kaēibiiō azīm rāniiō.skəraitīm gąm tašō

7.   *tat̰ θβā pərəsā arəš mōi vaocā ahurā*
kə̄ bərəxδąm tāšt xšaθrā mat̰ ārmaitīm
kə̄ uzəmām cōrət̰ viiānaiiā puθrəm piθrē
azə̄m tāiš θβā fraxšnī auuāmī mazdā
spəṇtā maniiū vīspanąm dātārəm

3.   I ask you this: tell me well, o Ahura! Who is, by engendering, the ancient father of Aṣa? Who has fastened here the road of the sun and there the road of the stars? Who is he who makes the moon wax then wane? Those are the things I want to know, o Mazdā, as well as others.

4.   ... Who, then, has held the earth down below and the clouds from falling? Who (has placed) here the waters and the plants? Who has harnessed the two fleet (coursers) for the wind and the clouds? Who, then, o Mazdā, has planted the pickets of [= to be used by] Vohu Manah?

5.   ... Which workman has placed here the light and there the darkness? Which workman has placed here sleep and there waking? Who has made morning, noon, and evening the moments that remind the one who desires of the object of his desires?

6.   ... Because the words I want to pronounce about the gods are such: "Ārmaiti, by her Good Thought (= Vohu Manah) and her ritual acts, supports Aṣa and has authority over you," for whom have you fashioned the milch cow, which makes (us) happy?

7.   ... Who fashions Ārmaiti, whom Vohu Manah admires, and provides her with ritual authority? Who has set up on the earth, one after the other, a son for the father? Anxious to receive answers to these (questions), I guide my favor toward you, o Mazdā, for my beneficent opinion is that you are the author of all these establishments.

This passage is one of the clearest of the entire corpus, and one may, without too great a risk, attempt a commentary on its meaning.

The initial act is one of engendering (3bb'), namely of Aṣa, which is the principle of organization of the universe, as well as, on the metaphorical level, of the tent. We know from other passages (Y.31.8, 45.4) that there was also engendering of Vohu Manah and Ārmaiti. Next, there is the arrangement of the two great cosmic oppositions, namely, of day and night and heaven and earth: Strophe 3 is devoted to the former. There is an opposition between the path of the sun on one hand (c) and the movement of the stars and the lunar phases on the other (c'-d'). After this, the divine work is represented as if it consisted of the laying out of a territory: the marking of the roads precedes the raising of the tent. Strophe 4 describes the organization of the three spaces: celestial, terrestrial, and intermediary: the last is mentioned through the setting in motion of the great atmospheric phenomena (dd'), an image that accompanies the road motif, while the secondary earthly opposition, water–plants, is grafted onto the primary opposition, earth–heaven (bb'). The opposition between heaven and earth is expressed in terms of upholding (*dərətā*). On the metaphorical level, the two fundamental oppositions are therefore the two distinct and complementary parts of the same motif. Heaven, which is the roof/ceiling of the tent, is not to be analyzed in terms of day and night, which means there is no distinction between the diurnal and nocturnal sky, and, indeed, there are no OAv. words for these two concepts. The opposition between day and night is a primary opposition parallel to that between earth and heaven, and not a secondary opposition derived from the dual nature of the sky. It is not part of the metaphor of the tent, but it is represented by the complementary image of the road, which renders the space around it part of the domestic area. The image of the tent is introduced at the point where the divine action consists in making the surface of the earth inhabitable. The contrasted pairs or triads in strophe Y.44.5—light and darkness; sleep and waking; morning, noon, and night—spring from the preceding oppositions and constitute their psychological version: their function is to provide the rhythm for the life of living beings. To these are devoted the following strophes: strophe 6 poses questions regarding the cow, strophe 7 regarding man and his piety (significantly, it is at this moment that the text passes into the present with the present injunctive *tāšt*). The planting of the pickets to be used by Vohu Manah (4 dd') takes place at the juncture in time when the cosmic action is finished and the organization of the living world begins. Now the turn has come to the two great exclusively ritual entities: Vohu Manah, but also Ārmaiti, who by means of supports and the authority she has over Ahura Mazdā, ensures for man the enjoyment of the cow (Y.44.6). Here we should note carefully that the act of planting the pickets and attaching the cord-work of Aṣa is not reserved for the gods. Not only do men contribute by their practices to preserving the order of the world, as it is said here and in Y.31.7, but their ritual activity is conceived on the model of the gods' founding act.: the ritual activity upholds Aṣa (Y.46.3): it either ties the last knot of the cord-work, or passes through the last turn of the road. Recall that in Y.48.7 it is the beneficent man (*nā spəntō*) who "ties" Aṣa. By a kind of circular logic, it is then up to the gods to make their contribution. The faithful sacrificer asks them to tie down the covering of Vohu Manah, and so ensure the final success of their undertaking (Y.48.7). In one of its aspects, the ritual is therefore the microcosm in which man, while helping to maintain the cohesion of the world, reproduces symbolically the cosmogonic work of the gods. And since this is possible only if the gods lend them their support, the ritual not only reproduces a model, but also seals the intimate complicity between gods and men.

Such, then, is the metaphor of the tent, which reveals the OAv. man's idea of the cosmogony, but also of the ritual, and in its application to the ritual we find its third point of importance. We know that the texts invariably contrast the follower of Aṣa (*aṣauuan-*) with the follower of the Druj (*drəguuaṇt-*). The exact semantic connection between *aṣa-* and its derived adjective *aṣauuan-* becomes clear from the opposition in Y.51.8 of *drəguuaṇt-* and the circumlocution *yə̄ aṣəm dādrē*: the *aṣauuan-* is "he who upholds Aṣa." The fundamental opposition between *aṣauuan-* and *drəguuaṇt-* is rooted in the metaphor of the cosmic hut.

A remarkable peculiarity of the Iranian image is its doubling. Next to the hut raised by Ahura Mazdā, which is structured by the principle of Aṣa and provides a model for the good ritual, there is the hut of the Druj, mentioned explicitly in two strophes: Y.46.6 *drūjō huuō dāmąm haēθahiiā gāṯ* "he will go to the pickets of the cord-work of the Lie" and Y.51.10 *huuō dāmōiš drūjō hunuš* "he is the son of him who plants the pickets of the Lie."

It is difficult not to correlate the existence of two distinct cosmic huts, one governed by the principle of Aṣa, the other by that of the Druj, with the disappearance of the opposition between the diurnal and nocturnal skies. The absence of the idea of "stretching," which is so important in Vedic, is the most noticeable effect of this disappearance: it is the very sign that the motif of the alternation between day and night, which are the two canvasses that the gods stretch successively over the world, is considerably modified. We see that it has left the metaphor of the hut to leave room for an opposition between the real structure (*aṣa-*) and the illusory, deceptive structure (*druj-*). Yet, the two oppositions are more or less the same. Ahura Mazdā and Aṣa are inseparably tied to the world of light. This is particularly clear in the key passages at the heart of the *Yasna Haptaŋhāiti*, at the beginning of the litany in *yazamaide*, on which see above and which presents the universe as having been established by Ahura Mazdā:

Y.36.6
sraēštąm aṯ tōi kəhrpə̄m kəhrpąm āuuaēdaiiamahī mazdā ahurā imā raocå
barəzištəm barəzimanąm auuaṯ yāṯ huuarə̄ auuācī
> "we recognize, o Ahura Mazdā, your body as the most beautiful of bodies: this sky, among the heights the one that is as high as the sun seen from down here."

That is, the luminous sky (*raocå*), from here (*imā*) to up above (*barəzištəm*), from the one who regards it down here (*auuācī*) up to the sun (*huuarə̄*), is the visible form of Ahura Mazdā (*tōi kəhrpə̄m*).

Similarly, in the next sentence (Y.37.1) and its prolongation in Y.37.4, Aṣa is presented as the patron of the celestial and intermediate worlds, of which the former is denoted by the name of light itself: *aṣəm ... hiiaṯ raocōŋhuuaṯ*. The association with the luminous sky bestows on both Aṣa and the form of Ahura Mazdā their character of resplendent beauty (Y.35.3 *aṣā srīrā*, Y.36.6 *sraēštąm aṯ tōi kəhrpə̄m*, Y.37.4 *aṣəm ... hiiaṯ sraēštəm*), defined by the adjective *srīra-* and its superlative *sraēšta-*. This beauty is not confined to the Haptahatic conception of Aṣa. The Gathic strophe Y.30.1 contains it, but in the form of *darəsata-* instead of *sraēšta-* (*aṣā.yecā yā raocəbīš darəsatā*), which, incidentally, reveals yet another difference in terminology between the two OAv. texts. This use of *darəsata-* shows that it is the celestial-diurnal nature of the great god and his principal entity which causes the verb *dars-* "see" to be applied to them so frequently: Y.28.5 *aṣā kaṯ θβā darəsānī*, Y.32.13 *yə̄ īš pāṯ darəsāṯ aṣahiiā*, Y.43.5 *hiiaṯ θβā* (= Ahura Mazdā) *aŋhə̄uš ząθōi darəsəm*, Y.45.8 *nū zīṯ cašmainī viiādarəsəm ... yə̄m mazdą̄m ahurəm*.

If the cosmogony is structured by the dichotomy between Aṣa, associated with the light of day, and the Druj, associated with the darkness of night, what about the ritual inspired by this cosmogony? Theoretically and logically, one would expect the good ritual to be that performed by day and the bad ritual that performed by night. In actual fact, however, we are confronted with a very difficult question: what were the concrete practices of the OAv. ritual? The allusive character of the *Gāθās* has always prevented specialists from agreeing on which practices were promoted and which rejected. Often it has been thought that the following passages contain a condemnation of the bloody sacrifice and the pressing of the soma/haoma:

Y.32.14
ahiiā ... nī kāuuaiiascīt̰ xratūš nī.dadat̰
... hiiat̰ vīsəṇtā drəguuaṇtəm auuō
hiiat̰cā gāuš jaidiiāi mraoī yə dūraošəm saocaiiat̰ auuō
> "when they accept to give their favor to the deceiver the kavis submit their intelligence to the one who makes the *dūraoša* (= the haoma?) favor blaze, when the cow is mistreated in order to be killed."

Y.48.10
... mūθrəm ahiiā madahiiā
yā ... karapanō urūpaiieiṇtī
> "the urine of this liquor (= the haoma), by which the karapans produce colic."

These two allusions are so unclear that it is possible to interpret them rigorously in three different ways:

1.   There is, in fact, a radical rejection of the practices in question: one must neither sacrifice the cow nor press the haoma.

2.   The text concerns only the excessive forms of these practices. The emphasis upon "mistreat" and "produce colic" is meant to indicate that the cruel forms of killing and the use of a toxic haoma, whose secondary effects are not mitigated by the addition of milk, are excluded.

3.   The sacrifice and the pressing are unreservedly part of the OAv. ritual, as they are of the Vedic Young Avestan rituals. The criticism of Y.32.14 and Y.48.10 is essentially aimed at the actors (*kauui, karapan*) and those who benefit from the ritual (*drəguuaṇt-*). I must add that translating *mūθrəm ahiiā madahiiā* by "filth, piss of a liquor" projects grammatical and semantic features of our modern languages into the OAv. text: *madahiiā* is a genitive and consequently not an apposition to *mūθrəm* but its determiner. We must translate "the urine of this liquor," whatever that means (the particular urine which the drinking of this liquor produces?).

Whatever the truth about the sacrifice and the pressing, some other rare and allusive passages are in agreement about either condemning the ritual by night or confessing the ritual by day. The definition of the adversary in Y.32.10 as "he who recites a very bad (hymn) in order to see with his eyes the cow and the sun" lends his sacrifice the purpose of making dawn reappear, which implies its nocturnal character. Y.43.16 describes the authority exercised by Zarathustra's ritual docility as "exposed to the sun." In Y.46.3 the intelligence of the sacrificers who bring Aša the support of existence—in the context of the cosmic hut!—receives, in apposition, the metaphorical designation "bull of the days." The expression reappears with a supplementary specification in Y.50.10: the "bull of the days" deserves to receive in his eye the lights of the sun, which are destined to pray to Ahura Mazdā. The Young Avesta still bears explicit testimony to the opposition between the sacrifice by day of the *ašauuan*s and the sacrifice by night of the *drəguuant*s: "Arəduuī Sūrā Anāhitā, what happens to the libations the *daēuuaiiasna drəguuant*s offer to you after the sun has set?" (Yt.5.94); "may my libations go into the light, not into darkness" (Nir.68).[12]

The diurnal character of the ritual implies necessarily that the OAv. sacrifice does not have the goal assigned to that of the adversary, namely, to ensure the daily reappearance of the sun. Its goal can be defined by the following passage:

Y.49.10
taṭcā mazdā θβahmī ā dąm nipåŋhē
manō vohū urunascā ašāunąm
nəmascā yā ārmaitiš

> "This is what you shelter in your house, o Mazdā: Vohu Manah, the *uruuan*s of the followers of Aša, and the homage by which there is Ārmaiti."

It is clear that we are in the middle of a passage dealing with eschatology. The preceding strophe affirms that the *mīžda-*, that is, "the recompense" and most often "the eschatological recompense," constitutes the ritual objective of the sons of Dəjāmāspa. The following strophe dooms the *drəguuant*s to an abominable existence after death. That Y.49.10 is, in fact, speaking about afterlife is confirmed by the parallel passage in Y.28.11, where the

---

12 [Ed. Sanjana, p. 278.]

verb "shelter" is qualified by *yauuaētāitē* "for eternity." We have here the relatively explicit description of the OAv. conception of paradise: Ahura Mazdā shelters in his house, for ever, Aṣa, Vohu Manah, the *uruuans* of those who uphold Aṣa, and the homage performed with Ārmaiti. This means that he receives as host the souls of the faithful with the positive characteristics of the cult which they render in life. The fate of the soul appears as the necessary result, not of an ethical behavior, which no text speaks about, but of the nature of the sacrificial practices. One of the essential characteristics of the OAv. system, is, in fact, this emphasis on the eschatological function of the sacrifice.

This is how it works: when the sacrifice is performed competently (*rādah-, arədra-*) by someone who acts in the appropriate manner (*dāθa-*) and at the right moment (*ərəθβa-*), the gods bestow authority upon them (*xšaθra-*). This authority is considered as the divine support par excellence (*rafəδra-, rafənah-*), and it is by exercising it that the sacrificer succeeds in opening the ritual road (*paθ-, aduuan-*) that permits gifts to go back and forth and be exchanged between gods and men (*maga-*). This mutual gifts are the various life forces (*jiiātu-*): *īš-* "vigor," *sauuah-* "swelling, opulence" *utaiiūiti-* "eternal youth," *təuuīšī-* "robust strength," *hauruuatāt-* "wholeness of the body," *amərətatāt-* "immortality." The exchange takes place within the actuality of the sacrificial ceremony conceived as a hospitality rite. The men receive the gods and make the offerings that reinforce their strength and guarantee their immortality, while the gods give men prosperity and longevity "for the material state, for this state." At the same time the sacrifice engages another mechanism of mutuality, that of hospitality: it forces the gods to receive in their home the *uruuan-* of the faithful after death, and it is the symbolic enactment of this future event. Eternal youth, vigor, wholeness and immortality are also the "spoils" (*āiiapta-*) of the "state of thought," that is, the state of life which the ritual expresses: symbolically won in the actuality of the sacrifice, they will be obtained concretely and definitively in the future reality, when the *uruuan-* arrives in the other world.

Offering immortality to the gods implies that the sacrifice contains something that is considered to be immortal. This could be the soma/haoma, as in the Vedic ritual, but it is not certain. Not only is it possible that the haoma ritual had been condemned, but also that the haoma was perhaps drunk by the faithful. To be on the safe side, let us say that something was either substituted for it or added as an offering of immortality. A number of OAv. passages can only be explained if they are seen in relation to a Greek testimony about the bloody sacrifice. Strabo, while describing the Iranian religion according to Herodotus and enriching it with the testimony of Oneisicritus and his own observations, reports that the victim is cut in pieces, which are laid out on the cover of ritual grass, but stresses that no part is offered to the gods, who only demand the soul. This conception, however, corresponds exactly to the one presupposed in the following YAv. passage:

Purs.33
gaospəṇta gaohudå baoδasca uruuānəm fraēšiiāmahi nazdišta upa θβarəšta raocå narš cašmanå sūkəm
> "o beneficent cow, o generous cow, we send your senses and your *uruuan* toward the nearest fashioned lights, that is, the light in the eyes of man."

Thus, the killing consists of sending the soul of the victim toward the lights, first those closest, which are the only ones mentioned in this fragment, then, probably, toward the sacrificial fire, the moon, sun, and stars, and the endless lights, where the gods dwell, So it seems it is the *uruuan* of the cow that constitutes the offering of immortality by which the sacrificer ensures the eternal breath of the gods:

Y.45.10
tə̄m ...
yə̄ ə̨nmə̄nī mazdå srāuuī ahurō
hiiaṯ hōi ašā vohucā cōišt manaŋhā
> "Ahura Mazdā, who is known by the breath that (Ārmaiti) bestows upon him through Aša and Vohu Manah."

For the same reason, it is the *uruuan* of the cow that crystallizes the entire eschatological symbolism of the ritual. The soul of the sacrificed cow reaches the divine world by the ritual path. In each ceremony, it is the replacement of the human *uruuan* in that it performs the journey into the beyond which one day it too must perform, reaching the goal which the faithful has chosen by his ritual practices: the lights of day and the tent of Ahura Mazdā. Incidentally, the idea of the soul of the victim journeying toward the gods is, of course, incompatible with certain ways of killing the victim. Some passages, in fact, seem to condemn suffocation, that is, the obstruction of the breath (Y.44.20). The word designating the shackle and the sprain that it causes (*rəma-*) is elevated to the rank of an evil allegory. The fact that the victim must remain unimpeded may thus explain the absence of an Iranian version of the *yūpa*, the sacrificial pole.

The texts are obscure on this point, but perhaps the *uruuan* of the cow is accompanied by the *daēnā* of the sacrificer on its journey. The *daēnā* is the mobile, journeying, part of the human soul, which ensures the connection between the *uruuan*, the soul inside the body which is liberated by death, and the *frauuaṣ̌i*, the celestial soul, and at death it proceeds to reunite them. It is tempting, and perfectly legitimate, to read into some strophes that the launching of a specialized part of the soul of the sacrificer onto the ritual road, accompanied by the soul of the victim, was expressed by the scene of a feigned death, either by pure mime or as an ecstatic practice. Thus, in Y.33.14, Zaraθuštra donates the mobility of his body (*uštāna-*) to Ahura Mazdā; in Y.43.4, he is qualified by *taxma-* "immobile, straight, fixed," and it is the same kind of attitude that is expected from Pourucistā in Y.53.3 (*təmcā.tū pourucistā*). Thus, this shamanistic aspect of the OAv. sacrifice would be the source of the motif of the journey into the beyond, which was later to play such an important part in the Mazdean tradition.[13]

The *Gāθās* and the *Yasna Haptaŋhāiti* are indeed liturgical texts in the strict sense; that is, they were composed exclusively to accompany a sacrificial ceremony. They go beyond the narrow frames of the liturgy only to the extent that they bear witness to a system of religious representations within which cosmogony, ritual, and eschatology are joined. In this system, the ritual occupies a central position. It is the place, whose actuality is constantly renewed, where the transition is produced in the cosmic sequence, or string, of events between the first and initial event, the cosmogonic act of the gods, which the second and central event, the ritual, reproduces symbolically and whose effects it guards, and the third and final event, the fate of man after death, which it guarantees. The symmetry about this pivot is imperfect, however. On one hand, there is the dawn of the world, on the other, the innumerable sequence of individual ends. We have to give in to the evidence, however: *pace* Mary Boyce,[14] the texts say strictly nothing about a last judgment or a renovation of the world, and they

---

13 Gignoux, 1979, pp. 41-79.
14 Boyce, 1984, pp. 57-75, refuted by Gignoux, 1986, pp. 334-346.

will say nothing about it for a long time. The OAv. universe is not expected to end, and the eschatology remains individual.

Thus, the very characteristic of the OAv. system is the permanent dichotomy that it introduces into the cosmic string of events, from the cosmogony to the end of each individual. There is a good and a bad cosmic hut, from which it follows that there is a good and a bad ritual, from which it follows that there is a good and a bad reception in the beyond. The principle that governs the good string of events is that of ordered structure (*aša-*), the principle that governs the bad one is that of deceptive structure (*druj-*). The Iranian religion therefore differs from the Indic one in two important respects. It presents a hardened, systematized version of the opposition between **r̥tá-* and **drujh-*: by associating the former with the day sky and the latter with the night sky, it lays down a rule for the functioning of the world that is not alternation, but radical separation. The term dualism is not too inappropriate for defining it, as long as one is clear about what one means by it. It is nothing less and nothing more than a cosmic dualism, since it is at work already in the cosmogony and everything follows from it. It is neither ethical nor psychological. The reason why scholars have entertained illusions in this respect is because of the importance that the Old Avesta—anticipating the Young Avesta—attaches to the opposition between two *maniius*—two "spirits," to use the conventional, though very inexact, translation. I have discussed the question of the two *maniius* on several occasions in the past,[15] which saves me from having to elaborate on its interpretation and its philological aspects here, which would be out of place. It seems to me that the verbal forms in the relevant passages exclude the possibility of there being a myth of the two "spirits" and that no usage of *maniiu-* satisfies the criteria for personification defined above (p. 20). In reality, the *maniiu* is an essentially human mental force. It is the act of thought that allows the faithful to make his ritual conform to the cosmogony. In the OAv. doctrine, the *maniiu* is one of the privileged tools of the religious knowledge. It is evident that the cosmogonic act lies beyond the reach of direct observation and corroboration; yet, man must get to know it, because he must organize his ritual according to this act. The *maniiu* is the *prise de conscience—* realization and awareness—that resolves this dilemma. Let us look, once

---

15 Especially Kellens, 1987, pp. 251-252.

more, at the cosmogonic passage Y.44.3-7. After having asked a series of questions about the originator of the cosmogony, the singer concludes by expressing a conviction that serves as answer (7 d'-e'), in the following, somewhat heavy, translation:

> "Anxious to (receive an answer to) these (questions) it is toward you that I direct my favor, o Mazdā, because, according to the beneficent realization I have had, it is you who have set about putting all these things in their places."

The *maniiu* is therefore the mental force that allows man to have an opinion about the cosmogony and to choose the ritual that follows from that opinion. Insofar as it is the instrument that joins the cosmogonic and ritual phases of the cosmic string of events, it plays an incontestable role in the dualist system, but a partial role only, and in any case the dualistic system is not based upon it. The basis of the Mazdean dualism is not the opposition between two *maniius*, whatever happens later in history, but the opposition between *aša-* and *druj-*.[16]

---

16 [More explicitly in Kellens, 1990, pp. 116-117: The OAv. *maniiu* is an essentially human mental force of a very precise type: it is the thought action that allows the faithful to have access to the religious knowledge. The gods' cosmogonic act is clearly located beyond man's ability to become directly aware of it, yet man must know about it, because he must organize his worship in the image of this act (see Kellens, 1989, pp. 65-78). The *maniiu* is the realization and awareness that solves the dilemma. We see from the last sentence of the cosmogonic passage in Y.44.2-7 that the *maniiu* is a mental intuition that allows man to have an opinion about Mazdā's cosmogonic act and to choose the ritual behavior that results from it. As an essential agent for the human attitude toward the gods, it plays a role in the dualistic system, without constituting its basis. This basis is the cosmic opposition between Aša and the Druj, the real Ordered Structure and the deceptive Ordered Structure: the *maniiu* is the opinion that determines man's allegiance to one or the other of these two principles. The thought act defined by *maniiu-* thus manifests itself visibly and officially in Zarathustra's worship. Recognizing that Mazdā is *spǝnta-*, Zarathustra, on behalf of the group he represents, experiences the obvious realization and awareness and chooses the good *maniiu*. In the framework of the Gathic liturgy, he is therefore the official human performer of the religious knowledge.]

In his *Zoroaster* (1952), Henning wrote that the Gathic dualism was "a protest against monotheism."[17] This famous formulation postulates, in hyper-abbreviated form, that Mazdaism is the result of a transition first from polytheism to monotheism, and then from monotheism to dualism. Since this dualism is not ethical-psychological, but cosmic, and although I shall present some reservations with regard to the meaning of "monotheism," I think we must reverse the formulation: OAv. "monotheism" appears to be a protest against dualism. To a world conceived of in terms of separation there corresponds naturally deities who are exclusively one or the other and even an omnipotent guarantor of the separation of the two cosmic strings of events. The preeminent role of Ahura Mazdā is evident. He dominates the deities of the good string of events, but he is also superior to whatever gods belong to the bad string of events. Not only was he the one who performed the primordial separation of the two strings of events, but his preeminence corresponds to the preeminence occupied by the good string of events and man's predilection for it.

The existence of a divinity at the top of a hierarchic scale, but far from being alone, has encouraged scholars to make a choice between the terms polytheism and monotheism. I do not intend to succumb to this alternative, which is just as absurd as that of the half-full or half-empty bottle. The term "henotheism" was also coined to deal with situations like this. Whatever etiquette dictates, it is better just to look and see how the system functions. The texts emphasize the importance of Ahura Mazdā. At the dawn of time he separated the two cosmic strings of events, and he is the sovereign of the good one. He is sole originator of the cosmogony: In 44.7 he is defined as *vīspanąm dātar-* "he who has put everything in its place"; he sets the pickets and attaches the cord-work of Aṣa. For all this, he ought to be the sole beneficiary of the ritual: this is the subject of Y.35. finally, he is the only host of the dead. In the Old Avesta, "paradise" is called explicitly the "tent" (*dam-*) of Ahura Mazdā, in the *Yasna Haptaŋhāiti* his "following" (*haxman-*). No other gods (e.g., the Entities or the *daēuuas*) are clearly seen to enjoy an equal rank.

Among these there are first of all the Entities (discussed above pp. 18ff.). In the *Gāθās*, Ahura Mazdā produces by engendering the three most important ones, who are also, in a certain sense, the only three. Those are

---

[17] Henning, 1952, p. 46.

the abstractions associated with his work: Aša, principle of the ordered structure of the cosmic hut, as well as Vohu Manah and Ārmaiti, the two ritual qualities that contribute to ensuring its permanent cohesion. In the *Yasna Haptaŋhāiti*, the entities are the geniuses of the various cosmic departments, and they are entitled to receive the *yasna* after Ahura Mazdā.

And the *daēuuas*: what is their place in this system? Etymologically the word corresponds to the title (*devá-*) of the Indic gods and is of good Indo-European stock (**deiu̯ó-*), but, in later Mazdaism, comes to denote demons. In the OAv. texts the position of the *daēuuas* is extremely unclear. first, we have no clue as to *who* they are. Their personal names are not mentioned, which means that we can only arbitrarily conjecture that the *daēuuas* are the gods who correspond to a given divinity of the *Veda* or the Young Avesta. Moreover, the criticism leveled against them is singularly nuanced. I would pay dearly to understand the meaning of Y.32.3 *at̰ yūš daēuuā vīspåŋhō akāt̰ manaŋhō stā ciθrəm / ... drūjascā pairimatōišcā*, which visibly situates the *daēuuas* with respect to abstractions antonymous to those incarnated by the entities (*akāt̰ manaŋhō* ≠ Vohu Manah, *drūjas°* ≠ Aša, *pairimatōiš°* ≠ Ārmaiti). But the expression remains incomprehensible, on one hand, because the semantic range of *ciθra-*, literally "that which is easily noted," is too large; on the other hand, because nowhere in Old Iranian do we find an analogous syntax: the verb "to be" (*stā*) qualifies the subject (*daēuuā*) by a substantivized adjective in the nom.-acc. sing. neut. (*ciθrəm*), the whole being qualified by an ablative phrase (*akāt̰ manaŋhō* etc.). We can always, as we have all done till now, give an *ad hoc* solution, but it is more honest and more correct simply to admit that we just do not understand the expression. The only thing that is certain is that the *daēuuas* are blamed for not knowing how to distinguish between the good and evil *maniiu* (Y.30.6) and for accepting the *aēnah-/énas-* (Y.32.4) characteristic of the ritual of those who sacrifice to them. We are unable to define precisely the discredit attached to this divine category: is it in the process of being demonized or just being pushed into the background? Note that later Mazdaism does not supply arguments for one or the other alternative, either, and, although the title is by then always derogatory, it is possible that the individuals themselves are still respected. Our present knowledge encourages us to remain cautious and respect the nuances of the text by presenting the situation in the following manner (which, at least, can not do any harm): the Old Avesta, contrary to the Young Avesta, does not qualify the *daēuuas* as *drəguuaṇt*——they are therefore not relegated to the bad string of events—but denies them the right to a *yasna*, which is the sole privilege of Mazdā and his entities.

Surrounded by one divine group that emanates from him and another that has radically lost prestige, Mazdā is superbly isolated at the top of the pantheon. This monotheistic garment of the OAv. religion has veiled its dualistic character. If Mazdā, the builder of the tent of Aṣa, had a direct adversary, who was the builder of the tent of the Druj, target of the bad ritual, and the host of hell, this dualistic character would be much clearer. Well, in my opinion, there can be no doubt that this sovereign of the bad string of events exists, even though he is only rarely alluded to. Two instances are quite certain. (1) Confrontation of Y.35.5 *huxšaθrō.təmāi bā aṯ xšaθrəm ... huuąnmahicā hiiaṯ mazdāi ahurāi* with Y.31.15 *yə drəguuāitē xšaθrəm hunāitī* shows that the *Gāθās* polemicize against a specific divinity, who is the target of the bad ritual, whom they refer to simply as *drəguuaṇt-*. (2) Y.51.10 *dāmōiš drūjō hunuš* attests explicitly the existence of someone who sets the pickets of the Druj. So what is the name of this god who organizes deception? With all due reservations, I would like to make the following remark: In Y.32.8 the name of Yima is mentioned in a context which, although incomprehensible, clearly attributes to him a negative action, but at the same time divine characteristics: he gives to the *maṣiia*s, that is, men as worshippers of the *daēuua*s, the favor, defined by the verb *xšnū*, which the divinity and the worshipper grant one another. Such a scheme, in which Mazdā, master of the good string of events, would be opposed to a god Yima, master of the bad one, would be possible if one imagines that the OAv. system did not evolve within the framework of the orthodox hierarchy illustrated by the Vedic pantheon, but within the framework of the "Yamic" hierarchy that Gérard Fussman reconstructed a few years ago.[18] Naturally, this is only conjecture, but, while exercising the greatest caution, we should also keep in mind this possibility.

It remains to ask ourselves, first, whether the OAv. system is an innovation or a dialect variant of the Indo-Iranian religion, and, second, if it is an innovation, whether it is the work of a man. We must therefore talk about Zarathustra.

---

[18] Fussman, 1977, pp. 21-68.

A problem of terminology:

gāθā- ~ hāiti- *and the unity of the* Gāθās

BEFORE WE SPEAK ABOUT the men mentioned in the *Gāθās*, we must agree on a point of terminology. In Western scholarship the term *gāθā-* is traditionally, but in a way that Humbach with good reasons termed "improper" (*ungenau*[19])—although he adopts it—used to designate the *hāitis*, or "chapters" of the *Yasna*. In contrast, the compiler who, at an indeterminable stage of the oral transmission of the text, arranged the Av. *Yasna* the way we now have it, used a precise terminology. He applied the name *gāθā-*, that is "song," to the various collections of different length that are characterized by the same meter. Thus, there are five *Gāθās*, named after their first one or two words: the *Ahunauuaitī gāθā* consists of Y.28-34; after the *Yasna Haptaŋhāiti* (Y.35-41) and a YAv. piece (Y.42), comes the *Uštauuaitī gāθā*, which covers Y.43-46; then the *Spəntāmaniiū gāθā*, which goes from Y.47 to Y.50; and finally the *Vohuxšaθrā gāθā* and the *Vahištōišti gāθā*, which occupy only one chapter each, Y.51 and Y.53, respectively. Within this framework, it would seem that the OAv. texts, including the *Yasna Haptaŋhāiti*, are simply arranged by decreasing length. Of the 72 *hāitis* making up the entire *Yasna* (Old and Young Avestan), the *Gāθās* occupy 17 and the *Yasna Haptaŋhāiti* 7, altogether 24 *hāitis*, which is the extent of the Old Avesta.

Western scholarship, however, has unfortunately become accustomed to using the term *gāθā-* for both the metrically homogeneous collections and the individual Gathic *hāitis*, with the result that the same author may talk about the "5 *Gāθās*," which agrees with the Young Avestan usage, and the "17 *Gāθās*," which is at complete variance with this usage.

The reason why this inconsistency has never bothered the specialists is that they have all been convinced that each *hāiti* is an independent poem. Bartholomae stated this as a fact: the corpus of the *Gāθās* consists of 17

---

[19] Humbach, 1959, p. 46.

independent pieces—the *hāitis*—collected into five greater units—the *Gāθās*—on the basis of the similarity of their meters.[20] This means that the *Gāθās* are only an artificial framework due to the vagaries of a compiler and which it would be totally useless to pay attention to. In this way the term *gāθā-*, empty of any useful meaning, could be used for other purposes and was substituted for *hāiti* (of a *Gāθā*). The hypothesis of the independence of the *hāitis* has never been properly argued and proved, however, only stated as a fact. Indeed, it is based upon an impression and a presumption. The *hāitis* of the *Uštauuaitī Gāθā* are so strongly characterized by the use of a refrain that it seems natural to consider them as autonomous wholes, and this impression has then been transferred to the entire corpus. The presumption is that every *hāiti* is a text connected with a signal event in Zarathustra's prophetic career. The hypothesis of the independence of the *hāitis* is therefore tied up with the notion that the *Gāθās* contain information about the life of Zarathustra, and so the scholars who most distrust the latter hypothesis are also the ones most skeptical of the former. For Darmesteter, for example, the independence of the *hāitis* was simply probable, nothing more.[21] Humbach, as he so often did, refuted the opinion of his predecessors, but refused to accept the consequences, namely, that, even though no biographical detail can be identified in the *Gāθās*, one must accept the hypothesis of the independence of the *hāitis* because it is completely impossible to find elements that connect them in their sequence.[22] This negative argument may or may not be true, but we should note that the relationship between two successive strophes of one and the same *hāiti* is also mostly impossible to grasp.

The only scholar to have resolutely defended the unity of the *Gāθās* is Marijan Molé (1963).[23] It is true that not all his arguments are compelling. Some are based upon an exegesis of the text and therefore stand or fall with the exegesis itself. Nevertheless, Molé's analysis is impressive whenever it is based upon formal aspects of the text, and these can be reduced to two general observations:

---

20 Bartholomae, 1905, p. V.
21 Darmesteter, 1892-3, p. xcviii.
22 Humbach, 1959, pp. 13-15.
23 Molé, 1963, pp. 176-189.

1. Every *Gāθā*, while following its own development and lending to each of its constituent parts an individual extent and tone, invariably and only once passes through some obligatory motifs. If there is in the *Gāθās* a compositional rule it is seen in the organic unity of each *Gāθā*. The most striking element is no doubt the fact that the final strophes of the first three *Gāθās* (those of more than one *hāiti*) consist of a number of varying formulas.

2. Within each *Gāθā* we occasionally find between two *hāitis* connecting elements that point to an artificial division. Thus, the passage about the "rule of allegiance" (*uruuata-*, OInd. *vratá-*) begins in Y.30.11 and ends in Y.31.6, the term itself being mentioned explicitly in Y.30.11, 31.1, 3. The passage centered around the verb *dā* goes from Y.33.14 to Y.34.3. A request for help (*auuah-*) in the form of a rhetorical question appears in the last strophe of Y.49 and the first of Y.50. Humbach pointed out these facts, but only to conclude that the person who made the arrangement used these elements to decide the order of the *hāitis*. That is theoretically possible, but not very probable. It would be too cute if a miraculous coincidence had provided a subtle compiler with pieces fitted like a puzzle. One would also have to point out a glaring contradiction in the mind of the organizer: why should he have made it appear as if these *hāitis* logically followed one another, while in other places he should have carefully obscured any relationship and made them seem completely independent? The repetition of words straddling two *hāitis* appears all the more intentional as it corresponds to two rhetorical techniques frequently found in the *Gāθās*: (1) the "lexical zone," in which a word is systematically repeated over several strophes, and (2) "lexical concatenation," by which the strophes are anchored to one another by the repetition of a word.[24] Still another sign of continuity is the following one of syntactic nature: the last verse line of Y.48.1 contains an aorist subjunctive (*vaxšat̰*), which can not be justified in an independent main clause, but is perfectly legitimate if the particle *at̰* that introduces this clause resumes the particle *zī* of the preceding strophe Y.47.6 (*hā zī ... vāurāitē*), for *zī* + aorist subjunctive in an independent main clause expresses exhortation.

Thus, the division into *hāitis* appears to be a completely artificial chapter division. So why did the organizer feel compelled to perform this dissection? It is best, I think, to admit that we do not know, but it is possible that it resulted from a wish to maintain a certain harmony of size

---

24 It was Hanns-Peter Schmidt who recognized and defined this procedure in Schmidt-Lentz-Insler, 1985, pp. 22-30.

and length between the Gathic *hāitis* and those of the rest of the *Yasna*. Without this dissection, each *Gāθā* would have represented a single *hāiti* of tens of strophes, which would have upset the balance of the ordering of the *Yasna*. Whatever the truth of the matter may be, in any case, we ought to use the organizer's terminology and call a *Gāθā* a *Gāθā* and a *hāiti* a *hāiti*.

The proper names

One motif which every *Gāθā*, whether consisting of one or more *hāitis*, must accommodate once, and only once, is the enumeration of a series of proper names. Each enumeration has its own rhetorical particularities and is more or less complete—the longest are those of the *Uštauuaitī* and *Vohuxšaθrā Gāθās*, the shortest that of the *Spəntāmaniiū*—but, generally speaking, we have the same names in the same order. They are the following, together with what the Mazdean tradition says about them:

Zarathustra (Zoroaster), properly Zaraθuštra, who composed and recited the text, sometimes mentioned together with one or more members of his family, either Maidiiōi.måŋha (a family relationship is actually not stipulated) or his daughter Pourucistā. Next come the *kauui* Vīštāspa, the king who received Zaraθuštra and converted, or would convert, to his message, and the two brothers Fərašaoštra and Dəjāmāspa, prominent persons at his court. Clearly, these traditional facts are grossly anachronistic, transposing as they do to the Iran of the year 1000 B.C.E. the institutions and atmosphere of the *Šāhnāme*. The *Gāθās* say nothing about the rank or function of the men mentioned in them. They describe no social organization and recount no event. At most, they give Vīštāspa the title of *kauui-*, on the basis of which scholars grant him royal rank. The only basis for such a reasoning, however, is the fact that in the Persian epic the heroes bearing the title of *kay* (from *kauui-*) are kings, but the epic typically fits the totality of old Iranian myths into a vast pseudo-history in the garb of a dynastic chronicle. All the other equivalents of *kauui-*—from OInd. *kaví-* to Manichean Middle Persian *kāw* via the Lydian loan-word *kave*—refer to somebody performing a religious function. On this basis, not only am I incapable of admitting that Vīštāspa is a king or anything like it, but I believe we have very good reasons—that is, grammatical reasons—for believing that he is, in the *Gāθās*, the son of Zaraθuštra. The traditional interpretation of Y.53.2 *kauuacā vīštāspō zaraθuštriš spitāmō fərašaoštrascā* is as a series of three coordinated names: Vīštāspa; then a son of Zaraθuštra referred to by the patronymic *zaraθuštri-* and the adjective *spitāma-*, but whose personal name is—strangely enough—not mentioned; and finally Fərašaoštra. Jared Klein's investigation of the Vedic use of the conjunction *-ca* and Eric Pirart's of the OAv. conjunction have unambiguously shown that in a coordination of three members there are only four possible configurations of the conjunction: (1) with each member (Acā Bcā Ccā), (2) with the last two (A Bcā Ccā), (3) only with the last (A B Ccā), (4) only with the first (Acā BC). The configuration Acā BCcā postulated for Y.53.2 is absolutely excluded because it is without parallel in all the old Indo-Iranian languages. The most elementary grammatical rules demand that our sequence consists of two coordinated members (AcāBcā), which implies that *zaraθuštri-* and *spitāma-* qualify *vīštāspō*.

Not only is this analysis the only one that satisfies the requirements of the syntax of coordination, but it is also the one which agrees best with the structure of the clearest and most explicit list, namely the one in the *Uštauuaitī*. There the distant relatives Friia, Tura, and possibly Uji are mentioned first in Y.46.12; then Zaraθuštra is mentioned twice, in Y.46.13 and 14, and Vīštāspa in Y.46.14, after the remote ancestors and before the mention of Zaraθuštra's family appurtenances: Haēcat.aspa and Spitāma in Y.46.15, giving the impression that these apply to both Vīštāspa and Zaraθuštra. If this analysis is correct, then the enumeration of the proper names presents two social groups.[25] The first is represented by Zaraθuštra and Vīštāspa and is defined by the patronymic *haēcat.aspāna-* and the epithet *spitāma-*, which lacks any formal mark of being a patronymic itself. The second is represented by Fərašaoštra and Dəjāmāspa and is characterized by the patronymic *huuō.guua-*. This leads us to ask two questions, to neither of which—unfortunately—I have a good answer.

first, what is the connection between the two groups? In theory, it can only be marriage ties, but which? As suggested to me by Clarisse Herren-schmidt, the Gathic group may have followed the rule of marriage with the crossed cousin on the mother's side, that is, a young man would preferably marry the daughter of the brother of his mother, a very common type of marriage in traditional societies, which Lévi-Strauss calls "generalized

---

25 Cf. Kellens-Pirart, 1988, pp. 4-12.

exchange" and which was practiced by the Achaemenids.[26] In that case, the sons of Haēcaṯ.aspa would give their daughters to the sons of Hugu(ua), which means that Fərašaoštra would be related to Zaraθuštra in the same way as Mardonius to Xerxes. An enticing scheme, but purely conjectural.

Second, to what social division do the patronymics *haēcaṯ.aspa-* and *huuō.guua-* correspond, on one hand, and the collective epithet *spitāma-*, on the other? We know, since the work of Emile Benveniste, that the OAv. society was apparently organized in four concentric circles, the names of which we render, for lack of better terminology, as "family, clan, tribe, nation," terms taken from ethnography.[27] The difficulty is that we do not know how the terms that situate an Old Avestan person in relation to his ancestors express his membership in one or another of these units. The only thing that is certain is that what I shall call the Gathic circle is composed of more than one family, since there is more than one common ancestor, and less than a nation, since elsewhere we are told that the nation he belongs to is hostile to him (Y.46.1).

If Vīštāspa is not king and Fərašaoštra and Dəjāmāspa not his ministers, is Zaraθuštra the author and reciter of the *Gāθās*? It is not so long ago that authoritative voices expressed a skepticism on this point that is today quite forgotten. Thus, Antoine Meillet pointed out that:

> "Yet, nothing proves that all the poems are by the same author. The fact that Zaraθuštra is often mentioned in the third person does not support the supposition that all the poems of the *Gāθās* are the work of the reformer himself."[28]

In addition to manifesting a healthy critical spirit, Meillet saw clearly what the difficulty was: the relationships between the name of Zaraθuštra and the grammatical persons are obviously complex and contradictory. Out of fifteen attestations of the name there are: (1) one certain attestation in the first person (Y.43.8); (2) one certain attestation in the second person (Y.46.14); (3) twelve certain attestations in the third person, of which one is in direct speech and so not relevant (Y.46.19); and (4) one obscure

---

26 Herrenschmidt, 1987, pp. 58-62.

27 Benveniste, 1932, pp. 117-134.

28 Meillet, 1925, pp. 14-15.

attestation which could be in the first or third person (Y.46.19). Looking more closely, however, we find that the situation is not quite as complicated as it seems and, in fact, allows no doubt: Zaraθuštra can on no account be the reciter, for the following four reasons:

1. It is, of course, admissible for the reciter to talk about himself in the third person, a procedure that is well attested in the *Rigveda*. The number of twelve third person references against only one first person reference is overwhelming, however. We would have to accept that the man who all through the text speaks in the first person (sing. or plur.)—"I, we"— systematically switches to the third person as soon as he mentions his own name. Let me also mention that it is not enough to gather the attestations of the name of Zaraθuštra in the third person, for who, other than Zaraθuštra, is the specific *man* (*nar-*) who features in several passages (especially Y.43.2-4) and who receives a certain number of specific and exclusively divine epithets?

2. It is also admissible, although quite odd, that one asks oneself a question in the second person with one's own name in the vocative (Y.46.14). We should note, however, that this direct address to Zaraθuštra precedes immediately that of the group of the Haēcat.aspa Spitāmas and that of Fərašaoštra and Dəjāmāspa. Logically, the reciter would seem to be addressing a series of persons beginning with Zaraθuštra. If Y.46.14 can not be uttered by Zaraθuštra, the same goes for the obscure passage Y.46.19, which concludes the section with the enumeration of the proper names.

3. The indisputable first person (Y.43.8) is attested in a sequence of eleven strophes (Y.43.5-15) beginning with *spəṇtəm at θβā mazdā mə̄ṇhī ahurā* "I think, o Mazdā, that you are *spəṇta* (beneficent)." This section is then explicitly represented as the direct speech of Zaraθuštra (Y.43.16). Thus, Zaraθuštra speaks once in the *Gāθās*, and his speech, carefully marked, contrasts with the rest of the text.

4. Last but not least, on three occasions the name of Zaraθuštra in the third person is directly opposed to a first person. That is obviously decisive: Y.28.6 *zaraθuštrāi ... ahmaibiiācā* "to Zaraθuštra and to us"; Y.49.12 *kaṯ tōi ašā zbaiieṇtē auuaṇhō / zaraθuštrāi kaṯ tōi vohū manaṇhā / yə̄ ... frīnāi* "what help do you have for Zaraθuštra, who requests it through Aša? What (help) do you have for me, who want to propitiate you by my good Thought (Vohu Manah)?"; Y.50.5 *mąθrānē ... auuaṇhā ... yā nå x^vāθrē dāiiāṯ / yə̄ mąθrā vācəm mazdā baraitī / ... nəmaṇhā zaraθuštrō* "For the

maθrān Zaraθuštra, who speaks with respect, this help by which he places us in well-being."

If Zaraθuštra is not the reciter, who is? The liturgical recitation of the *Gāθās* was probably a specific ritual task, whose corresponding title we do not know for sure. As for the *zaotar-* (OInd. *hótar-*) mentioned in Y.33.6, who is often identified with Zaraθuštra and so also the reciter, he lacks a first person reference. In Y.48.9, the reciter appears to define himself as *saošiiaṇt-*, as the first person *vaēdā* "I know" is underscored by the exclamation in the optative *vīdiiāt saošiiąs* "may the *saošiiaṇt-* know!" This term denotes collectively those who participate in the sacrificial activity and means literally he who will offer and receive the *sauua(h)-* "swelling," one of life's prosperities that is exchanged during the sacrifice. It is not, however, a title specifically connected with the recitation of the text.

Under these circumstances, can Zaraθuštra be regarded as the author of the *Gāθās*? In my opinion, the question of an author is meaningless. The *Gāθās* do not stand forth as the work of one man, but as the expression of an entire religious group. They are not the work of a personality, but a product of a mentality. Naturally, somebody must have actually composed them, but must we really ask whether it was the most important person in the Gathic circle, one of its outstanding companions, or an obscure individual who was skilled in the art of verse-making? One possible conjecture would be to base ourselves upon the title *kauui* borne by Vīštāspa. Vīštāspa poet instead of Vīštāspa king? The evidence is very fragile, as we can not prove that *kauui* meant strictly "poet" in Old Avestan, although it is possible. The question of how many authors there were is correspondingly untreatable. What is the point of multiplying an already evanescent author?

The people mentioned by name in the *Gāθās* appear both as representatives of a social group and as actors in the ritual. The first aspect emerges from the systematic use of patronymics and the group name *spitāma-*. As for the second aspect, it is defined explicitly by the verb *yazəmna-* (OInd. *yájamāna-*), which concludes and resumes the enumeration of the proper names in the *Vohuxšaθrā Gāθā* (Y.51.20). The men of the *Gāθās* are therefore—to recapitulate while leaving out details that, anyway, we do not understand—chiefs and sacrificers. The foremost among them is Zaraθuštra, whose prominence is marked by three formal facts. He is always mentioned at the head of the list; he returns frequently at the end of the list, so that he frames the entire section; and, in each of the multi-*hāiti Gāθās*, he is mentioned once, and once only, outside the enumeration of proper names. Zaraθuštra's ritual functions are unmatched. Even if he is not the "I" of the *Gāθās*, he is given the right to speak, and he is presented as an exceptional singer: Y.29.8 *huuō nā vaštī ašāicā / carəkərəθrā srāuuaiieṅhē* "he wishes to make us hear, o Mazdā and Aša, celebrations"; Y.31.19 *vīduuå ... / ərəžuxδāi vacaṇhąm xšaiiamnō hizuuō vasō* "the knowing one who masters at will his tongue for the correct enunciation of the words"; Y.50.6 *yə mąθrā vācəm mazdā baraitī / uruuaθō ašā nəmaṇhā zaraθuštrō* "Zaraθuštra, the *mąθrān* who speaks with Aša and respect." According to the same strophe, he is *dātā xratōuš hizuuō* "he who ensures the efficiency of the tongue" and the reciter begs for his teaching. He pronounces in person the eleven strophes Y.43.5-15.

Zaraθuštra is characterized by a series of four or five adjectives which are otherwise only applied to the ritual fire and/or Ahura Mazdā. Let us leave aside *hudānu-* (OInd. *sudánu-*), too rare for us to understand its semantic range. There remain two epithets that refer to his ritual talent: like the fire, he is *arədra-* "(ritually) competent" and *ahūm.biš*, which means that he lends his ritual health, contrary to his opponents, who make their ritual sick (Y.30.6). The epithet *θβāuuaṇt-* "who is with you" points to his special relationship with Ahura Mazdā, accentuated by the epithets *hudāh-* "generous," which denotes the participation in the divine universe, and *spəṇta-* "beneficent," which denotes the very quality of the great god.

Zaraθuštra bears an official title: *mąθrān-*, OInd. *mantrín-*, literally, "he who possesses the *mąθra*s." One must be well aware, however, that OAv. *mąθra-* is used in a way that distinguishes it radically from its Indic equivalent, in that it does not denote a human word, the poem, but a divine word. The gods make known their will by a certain number of words, which all have their specific, technical, name. Among them, there are the *mąθra-* "formula" and *sāsnā-* "lesson," which are always closely associated. Both come from Ahura Mazdā. He made them in accordance with Aša (Y.29.7), and Zaraθuštra's characteristic feature is that he, and only he, is able to hear these words (Y.29.8). The text uses the word "hear" (*guš*), and not "listen to" (*sru*), lending Zaraθuštra not piety, but a special kind of obedience, a particular function, namely that of transmitter between gods and men. He causes the *mąθra-* to be applied, be realized (*mąθrəm varz*), and he pronounces the divine teaching that allows the ritual path to be

opened (Y.43.3). Zaraθuštra is he who knows (*vīduuāh-*) a divine knowledge that he transmits to men. He plays an essential role in accessing this
religious knowledge, which I spoke about earlier and which allows men to
adjust their ritual to the great divine acts situated beyond their reach. The
hāiti Y.43 is particularly clear in this respect. By recognizing Ahura Mazdā
as *spəṇta*, Zaraθuštra obtains, on behalf of the group he represents, the
realization and awareness that is needed to choose the good *maniiu*. Within
the framework of the Gathic system he is the human who actually receives
and possesses this religious knowledge. But this has another actor, as well:
the ritual fire, to whom the same terminology assigns the same knowledge
and the same ability to teach, to the extent that in some (perhaps
intentionally) obscure or too allusive strophes it is impossible to decide
whether they are about the fire or about Zaraθuštra. The two make a couple,
united in one and the same function, namely, to ensure an open connection
between the divine world and the human ritual. They gain understanding of
nature and the divine will, the teachings aimed at men, and, in return, make
apparent to the gods men's realization and awareness: the fire by the magic
of its light and heat, Zaraθuštra by the triad thought–word–action, which he
performs. They are the two who ensure the ritual transition.

It is on this point that we might locate an essential difference between the
Gāθās and the *Yasna Haptaŋhāiti*. In the former, the ritual transition is en-
sured by the fire and a human protagonist, indistinguishable by terminology.
In the latter, the fire is alone, while the reciters bestow on one another the
title of *mąθrān-* (Y.41.5). The Gathic ritual has a sacralized human star
player, while the Haptahatic one is collective and anonymous. It can hardly
be by chance that the name of the circles of social appurtenance has only a
metaphoric value in the *Yasna Haptaŋhāiti*, where the only one mentioned is
the one the sacrificers make around the ritual fire (Y.36.1): *ahiiā θβā āθrō
vərəzə̄nā ... pairijasāmaidē mazdā ahurā* "we serve you, o Ahura Mazdā,
by forming the clan of this fire." To the Gathic motif of the evocation of an
actualized social group there corresponds in the *Yasna Haptaŋhāiti* the
chapter dedicated to the consecration of the ritual fire. These two moments
of the recitation are similarly associated with the ritual phase that is referred
to by the technical term *yāh-* and even constitute this phase.

Should Zarathustra be regarded as the inventor of the particularities of the
OAv. doctrine? I do not see how, at the current stage of our knowledge, we
could deny the innovating character of this system. It is too particular

among the various old Indo-Iranian religions, especially by the way the divine personnel is treated, with the elevation of Ahura Mazdā and the criticism of the *daēuuas*. On the other hand, we can neither regard it as certain that the *Gāθās* reflect the first steps of a new system, nor that this innovation is the fruit of a personal speculation. There *is* one argument in favor of the hypothesis that the *Gāθās* reflect the first steps of a new system, and it is a strong one: the existence of adversaries. These are situated at the head of the *daxiiu* "nation," and this definite positioning in the structure of the circle of social appurtenance seems to bear decisive witness to their reality. Yet, the consequences of this witness must be seen relatively. Not only are the adversaries absent from the *Yasna Haptaŋhāiti*, but we must also not forget that the adversary is altogether a doctrinal necessity for a dualistic system. If there is a bad string of events it must have its partisans, and we do not know who are the adversaries of the Gathic circle: are we talking about people resisting the central innovation of the doctrine or another Mazdean school, rejected because associated with the Lie? If this is the case, then the innovation can be so old that it can be considered as a basic constituent of the Iranian religion itself.

As for the question of a personal origin of the innovation, I will be more precise. It is a scenario that seems to me not very probable, for the confrontation of the *Gāθās* and the *Yasna Haptaŋhāiti*, now that they have been recognized as more or less contemporary texts, shows that the OAv. doctrine is not homogeneous, but split into different schools. What is more, if the characteristic feature of the OAv. innovation is indeed the transition from the concept of alternation to that of separation as the organizing principle of the world, we are bound to recognize that this evolution does not seem to correspond to a personal philosophical reflection, but to a movement of the mythical thought. The Old Avesta is perhaps neither the founding text of a system nor a work bearing the signature of its author. It retains one merit, however, and not a small one at that, namely, to have so well expressed a religious thought that its position as the liturgical text of Mazdaism has not been shaken for several millennia. This merit is that of two schools, the Gathic and the Haptahatic, both of which—the one no less than the other—produced its constituent parts. The fact that the *Gāθās* recognize explicitly the social and religious preeminence of duly named persons does not at all imply that they played a more important part in the development of Mazdaism. In fact, aside from the legend of Zarathustra, the influence of the *Yasna Haptaŋhāiti* on the Young Avesta is noticeably greater than that of the *Gāθās*. I am even no longer as certain as I was in the introduction to the *Textes vieil-avestiques* of the historicity of the men of the *Gāθās*.[29] I am certainly not convinced of the opposite, but I now think that it is reasonable to entertain some doubt on this point. I invite you, at the end of these conferences, to review the indications that the proper names mentioned in the *Gāθās* are not those of real men but emblematic names for which each group, in the liturgy, could substitute those of their own representatives or in which they could recognize them. There are four such indications, listed here in increasing order of strength of argument:

1. Two names out of the nine that constitute the onomastic corpus of the *Gāθās* are metrically inadequate: *huuōguua-* counts three syllables instead of the two required by the etymology; *spitāma-* counts three syllables instead of the four required by the etymology. In fact, the only explanation of this word that comes readily to mind is as a *bahuvrīhi*, meaning "who possesses white force," from *spita-* "white" plus *ama-* "(offensive) force." The word ought therefore to be read as **spita'ama-* with hiatus between the two members of the compound. These two irregularities suggest that the Gathic proper names occupy a metrical slot which was originally not made for them, but we are dealing here with not very solid facts. Note, for instance, that in the Rigveda, the patronymic *ātithigvá-*, which has the same second member as *huuōguua-* counts, inexplicably, five feet, one more than expected. As for *spitāma-*, it is perhaps preferable to regard it as being of unknown etymology.

2. As I already pointed out in the introduction to *Textes vieil-avestiques*,[30] the names of the brothers Fərašaoštra and Dəjāmāspa show a clear concern for stylization: the second members of the two compounds together with that of *huuōguua-* make up the triad cow–horse–camel, and the first members are antonyms: *fəraša-* corresponds to OInd. *pŕkṣá-* and *dəjāma-* to *kṣāmá-*, which means that Fərašaoštra is "he who possesses juicy camels" and Dəjāmāspa "he who possesses dried-out horses." This looks very much like the invention of a playful author. It is obviously possible to attribute it to the father of the two men, which is what I did, but the following points make us hesitate.

3. We know that in the Mazdean tradition, from the Young Avesta onward, Zaraθuštra's father's name is Pourušāspa. This name is not found in the

---

29 Cf. Kellens-Pirart, 1988, pp. 4-12.
30 Kellens-Pirart, 1988, pp. 4-5.

Gāθās, where Zaraθuštra's paternal ancestry is defined by the patronyms *haēcat̲.aspa-* and *haēcat̲.aspāna-*. In the introduction to *Textes vieil-avestiques*,[31] I analyzed these two words—as I now think, erroneously—by assuming that *haēcat̲.aspa-*, applied to the men of Zaraθuštra's generation, was a patronymic with *guṇa* as its only distinctive mark, while *haēcat̲.aspāna-*, derived from the former by means of the suffix *-āna-* and, applied to Zaraθuštra's daughter, was a pro-patronymic. This interpretation leads to two anomalies: it carelessly bestows on the patronymic the strict meaning "son of," and it presupposes as the underlying proper name **hicat̲.aspa-*. The first member of this name does not, however, correspond to any present stem of the root *hic*, OInd. *sic* "to pour, sprinkle." Therefore, today I prefer to regard *haēcat̲.aspāna-* as the patronymic and *haēcat̲.aspa-* as the proper name from which it is derived. This means that in Y.46.15 *haēcat̲.aspā* is the plural of the proper name used to denote the sons of Haēcat̲.aspa, in the same way that OInd. *rudrā́ḥ* "the Rudras" denote the Maruts. Thus Humbach's hypothesis is rehabilitated, taking *haēcat̲.aspa-* as "he whose horses are besplattered (with mud),"[32] where the first member *haēcat̲*, corresponding to a thematic present stem *haēca-* (OInd. *sécate*) as opposed to **hiṇcat̲* (OInd. *siñcáti*) active, is used in the middle function of the verb. This does not mean that the parallel in *Rigveda* 4.43.6 *síndhur ha vāṃ rasáyā siñcad áśvān* "the river waters your horses with spray" is irrelevant, but it must be adapted from the point of view of its middle voice. Within the framework of this analysis we are no longer obliged to regard *haēcat̲.aspa-* as the name of Zaraθuštra's father—it could be that of a more remote ancestor—but we should notice the curious fact that *haēcat̲.aspa-* and *pourušāspa-* could be approximately synonymous if we understand the former as "he who has besplattered horses" and the latter as "he who has dirty horses." The question then becomes: are there two Avestan traditions about the name of Zaraθuštra's father, which agree on its meaning but diverge with regard to its form?

4. The last point, which is also the most impressive one, comes from the last *Gāθā* (Y.53). This brief and mostly incomprehensible text with its sophisticated metrics presents three converging particularities:

    a. A women is mentioned in the enumeration of the proper names, Pourucistā, a Spitamid, descendent of Haēcat̲.aspa-, and the youngest daughter of Zarathustra, to whom a central ritual part seems to be assigned.

    b. The liturgical function of the text is clear: the reciter speaks in the function of paranymph in a marriage ceremony. As such, he addresses the

---

31 Ibid., p. 8.
32 Humbach, 1973, pp. 96-97.

> "young women ... and you (all)" (*kainibiiō ... xšmaibiiācā*). There is no
> reason for thinking that this "you (all)" is an exception to the OAv. rule
> that the reciter addresses himself exclusively to the gods and, for rhetorical
> effect, his adversaries, but never to the "public."
>
> c. This *Gāθā* also contains the only mildly titillating passage of the Old
> Avesta (Y.53.7). Something, called *āžu-* of unknown meaning, is said to
> go back and forth between the thighs. The author, in an ambiguous ex-
> pression, plays on words by confusing "the hole which must be pierced"
> (*vīzaiiaθā magəm*) and "the sacrificial exchange which must be incited"
> (*ahiiā magahiiā*).

All this clearly invites us to regard Y.53 as corresponding to a ritual of
hierogamy. The future spouses are the male gods, invited to unite sexually
with the young women of the Gathic circle. These apparently personify
those of the ritual abstractions that are of feminine gender, or the *daēnā*s of
the sacrificers. Of these young women, Pourucistā is the prototype. Let us
pay careful attention to her name, however, which has always been thought
to be a *bahuvrīhi* from *pouru* "much" and *cistā-* = *cisti-* "intuition, idea,"
that is, "she who has many intuitions." This is impossible, however, for the
suffix *-tā-* is exclusively secondary. The only way to salvage the traditional
interpretation is to posit a derivative **cisti-tā-* reduced to *cistā-* by hap-
lology, like the frequent *amərətāt-* for *amərəta-tāt-*. But what would be the
function of a derivative in *-tā-* from a noun in *-ti-*? In fact, *cistā-* is easily
explained as the feminine of the (passive) verbal adjective in *-ta-* (the ppp.)
of *cit-* "to mark, notice." Thus, *pourucista-* would be a very common kind
of compound, a *tatpuruṣa* with a prior member in instrumental function
depending on a ppp. as the second member, meaning "she who is noticed by
many," maybe even "she who is noticed by the many (gods)." And is it
only a coincidence that the participant in a marriage ritual, whether
hierogamic or not, has a name which refers to her power of seduction? In a
case like this, it is difficult to get rid of the impression that the name was
made for the function of its bearer.

Thus the Gathic onomastics reveals itself as metrically inadequate,
stylized, artificial, and based upon ritual functions. This conclusion does
not reassure us about the historicity of the named members of the Gathic
circle. The hypothesis of conventional names can not be discarded by a
sleight of hand.

But in spite of everything, even if Zarathustra and his companions were no more than the Cleandros and Orgon[33] of the *Gāθās*, still the profound unity of the text can not be doubted. The *Gāθās* and the *Yasna Haptaŋhāiti* are extremely close to one another in space and time, revealing only minor divergences in language and doctrine. Even greater is the intimacy between the individual *Gāθās*, where it is impossible to detect any significant individual peculiarities. We must admit that they were composed in the same place, at the same time, and by the same school. Their threefold linguistic, doctrinal, and rhetorical unity puts this beyond doubt. We have here a coherent corpus, which differs from all the rest of the *Avesta*, namely the Old Avesta.

---

33 [Characters of the Italian Commedia dell'Arte.].

Yima and Death

(1988)

IN AN ARTICLE devoted to the Avestan legend of Yima, which I wrote in early 1980 for the *Mélanges Duchesne-Guillemin*, I concluded that it was not possible to determine from what original state of the myth and by which process India and Iran had come to situate their homonymous primeval hero in exactly opposite relations to death. For lack of documentation, comparative mythology has not been able to provide an answer to the question, which is directly connected with that of the origins of the innovating religious system that marked the beginning of Iranian history. We can only assume that the discovery of the realm where Yima receives the souls of the dead and the construction of the *vara*, in which Yima saves the living species from the great winter, both derive from the same original motif. In general, one has always been inclined to regard Iran as the innovator, although without providing definitive proof. Had not Iran manifested its powerful capacity for reformative speculation through the elaborate development of Mazdaism? As a matter of fact, since 1980 two studies have brought very strong arguments in support of this hypothesis, by uncovering the traces of an ancient relation between Yima and death. Jacques Duchesne-Guillemin (1980) showed that the horn (*suβrā-*) of Yima must originally have played a role in the governing of the society of souls. This seems a foregone conclusion, since the horn finds its proper place between the flute (*nā́ḍi-*) of Yama mentioned in the Rigvedic hymn X.135.7 and the trumpet (*ṣūr*) of Isrāfil, both the name and motif of which was taken up in the Muslim tradition. On the other hand, Bruce Lincoln (1982) pointed out that the way in which Yima constructed the *vara*, by mixing earth and water, corresponds exactly to the idea various peoples of Indo-European origin have of paradise: a universe enclosed by clay walls, which is a mythological transposition of the closed space of the tomb. I think that the Mazdean mythology has preserved, although masked, still another element of Yima's relation with death. Before I proceed to analyze it, let me say that, as my first thoughts on Yima were offered to Jacques Duchesne-Guillemin, I am happy to present the second as homage to another great scholar of Belgian origin.

It is well known that Mazdean Iran had a very different idea of the next world than Vedic India. Here it is not represented as a realm of souls but as a place of judgment, where everybody receives the salary for his actions. The souls are not submitted to the authority of the first man to have "lived" death, but appear, as soon as they arrive, before a tribunal presided over by at least Ahura Mazdā, Vohu Manah, good Vāiiu, Miθra, Sraoša, and Rašnu. Nevertheless, certain motifs of the Vedic idea can be seen. In an Avestan fragment (Aog.77-81), the passage from life to death is the "road of implacable Vāiiu" (*pantå ... yō vaiiaoš anamarždikahe*), an image that corresponds to the road that Yama was the first to find (RV.10.14.1 *ánu bahúbhyaḥ pánthām anuspaśanám*). The two dogs that guard this road according to RV.10.14.11 (*yáu te śvánau ... pathirákṣī* "your two dogs that guard the road") also appear in the Avesta. They are mentioned in V.13.9 (*spāna pəšu.pāna* "the two dogs that guard the bridge"), and in V.19.30 they accompany the young woman-*daēnā* who comes to meet the soul (*hāu srīra ... spānauuaiti* "the beauty with the dogs"). Thus, in the entire Mazdean tradition, from the *Gāθās* to the theological Pahlavi books, the critical point of access to paradise is a bridge which has no equivalent in the Indian tradition. This image is not a variant of that of the road, because it illustrates the last formality to be observed before entering into the sojourn of the blessed. At the end of the road is situated the tribunal of the gods who, according to the merits of the deceased, grant or deny the passage of the bridge. The bridge is called *cinuuatō pərətu-*, where the word for "bridge" (*pərətu-*) receives the genitive complement *cinuuatō*, or, in some late passages, *cinuuat.pərətu-*, a *tatpuruṣa* compound. We are therefore dealing not with the "*cinuuat* bridge," as one can read all too often, but the "bridge of the *cinuuant-*." The word *cinuuant-* is an active present participle in the function of an agent noun (of the same type as *saošiiant-*) and seems to denote a mythical being not otherwise identified and who has left no traces elsewhere. Up till now the word has been explained in three different ways:

1. Bartholomae (1904, cols. 596-597) derived *cinuuant-* from [1]*ci* (col. 441: [1]*kay* "legere" ["to gather"]) and translated the expression as "Brücke des Scheiders." Thus we are dealing with "the bridge of the separator," he who separates the good from the evil.

2. Nyberg (1937, p. 205) derived it from the root *ci* "to notice," which is attested in Vedic, and postulated "the bridge of the scrutinizer."

3. Bailey (1939, pp. 115-116) based his interpretation on [2]*ci* "pay in retribution for a sin" (Bartholomae, 1904, col. 464: *kāy* "repay" and translated "the bridge of the exactor."

Thus all three roots *ci* attested in Indo-Iranian were successively invoked, each of them providing a meaning which could seem appropriate for defining the ultimate obstacle separating the soul from paradise. There is a grammatical clue, however, which allows us to choose between the three. The participle *cinuuant-* is derived from a present stem *cinao-/cinu-*. This fact alone suffices to exclude Nyberg's and Bailey's solutions. The root *ci* "to notice" is not attested in Iranian and does not form a present stem of the required type till in Epic Sanskrit. The root *ci* "to repay" has a thematic present in Indian *cáya-*, which is exclusively middle, and in Avestan a reduplicated present *cikaē-/cici-* exclusively active. From a grammatical point of view, Bartholomae's hypothesis is the only plausible one. We can not accept it without reservations, however. Bailey objected with full right that the translation "the bridge of the separator" was based on the verb *vī-ci*, with preverb *vī-*, which means "to distinguish between" and which in the active takes two accusatives (Y.46.17 *yə̄ vīcinaot dāθəmcā adāθəmcā* "he who distinguishes the pious and the impious") and in the middle an accusative dual (Y.30.6 *aiiå nōit̰ ərəš vīšiiātā daēuuācinā* "between those two the *daēuuas* above all did not choose rightly"; also Y.30.3). The simple verb *ci*, from which *cinuuant-* is necessarily derived, is not attested in Indian and poorly in Iranian. It appears in a fragment which is so badly transmitted that it is incomprehensible (Her.1) and the present stem *caiia-* can be restored by conjecture in three parallel phrases in a good *yašt* (Yt.13.11, 22, 28), a form probably derived from the root aorist *caē/ši-* by secondary thematization (cf. Kellens, 1984b, p. 333). It is, however, very

much alive in western Middle Iranian. Manichean Middle Persian has *cy-* <
**caya-*, and both Manichean Middle Persian and Parthian have *cyn-* <
**cinu-* (cf. Ghilain, 1939, p. 85), still found in modern Persian as *cīdan* (cf.
Henning, 1933, pp. 181-202). The meaning "to gather, accumulate" or,
more exactly, "to pile up" is confirmed by the Sasanian inscriptions, where
we have Middle Persian *cyt'k* < **citǎka* = Parthian *šyty* "heap of stones"
(Gignoux, 1972, pp. 21, 65).

Thus *cinuuatō pərətu-* can only be "the bridge of the piler." The "piler"
denotes the one who builds the bridge by putting stones upon stones, and it
is difficult to see who it could be other than the equivalent of the Indian
Yama. In this way it appears that, in the Iranian tradition too, Yima played
a role in the inauguration of the sojourn of the dead. When was this part
taken away from him and why? Did the editor of the *Gāθās* still recognize
him in the *cinuuaṇt-* of the expression *cinuuatō pərətu-*? And what about
the authors of the various parts of the Young Avesta? Questions without
answers. At any rate we should note and add to the repertory gathered in
my article in the *Mélanges Duchesne-Guillemin* (1980) the fact that Yima
played a role in the setting up of the next world acting as a builder. While
his Indian homologue, probably by innovation, only investigated the road as
a scout, Iranian Yima was the actual builder of the road to paradise, in the
same way that he was to build the *vara* later.

The Speculative Ritual in Ancient Mazdaism

(1994)

EVERYTHING WE KNOW about the ancient Iranian liturgy comes from the Avesta, the sacred book of Mazdaism.[1] Let me recapitulate briefly some facts. The Avesta, which the French Anquetil-Duperron uncovered in India in the middle of the 18th century among Mazdean communities who had emigrated from Iran during the Islamization of the country, came into our hands through the intermediary of a relatively late manuscript material (none of the manuscripts goes beyond the middle of the 13th century C.E.). By paleographic analysis it has been possible to date the invention of the alphabet destined to write down the Avesta to the time between the 4th and 6th centuries in Sasanian Persia. The text, or at least some parts of it, had until then been transmitted orally, carefully and reliably, in the same way that the vast Vedic literature had been transmitted in neighboring India (we are therefore dealing with a traditional Indo-Iranian technique of preserving texts). The Avesta is not a homogeneous book, however. We must at least make an elementary distinction between the Old Avesta and the Young Avesta, which form two strongly contrasting parts. The Young Avesta is composed in a language that was used for a very long time, first as a living language, then as a scholarly language. At a very vague and rather

---

1 *The speculative ritual in ancient Mazdaism* reproduces opinions put forward in *Les textes vieil-avestiques* I-III (1988, 1990, 1991) and in *Zoroastre et l'Avesta ancien* (1991). The sections about time, the complementarity of seeing/hearing, and the gods to whom the sacrifice is addressed are new. The last point was also discussed more fully in *Le panthéon de l'Avesta ancien* (1994).

conventional estimate, the oldest Young Avestan texts are contemporary with the earliest Achaemenid inscriptions (end of the 6th century B.C.E.), and the latest ones are contemporary with the invention of the alphabet, which means that the Avesta was composed over a period of about a millennium.

The Old Avesta consists of a metrical part (the five *Gāθās* or "songs") and a part in prose (the *Yasna Haptaŋhāiti* < *Hapta-hāti* or "sacrifice in seven chapters"). The Old Avesta is a very short text (let us say about 50 pages), as well as very homogeneous, in contrast to the Young Avesta. There appears to be not the least trace of any significant linguistic development between the two Old Avestan texts. It is, for instance, impossible to tell whether one of the *Gāθās* is older than any of the others or if the *Yasna Haptaŋhāiti* is older or younger than the *Gāθās*. One has a strong impression that the entire ancient corpus originated at a precise time. It is very difficult to specify this time and quite impossible to locate the place of origin of the texts (all one can say is that they probably were not composed in western Iran, that is, Persia or Media). On the basis of the astonishingly archaic character of Old Avestan as opposed to Young Avestan and Old Persian, most scholars today wisely put a lapse of about four centuries between the two groups and thus date the Old Avesta to about 1000 B.C.E. (which is still, probably, too timid).

From Christian Bartholomae (1905) to Jacques Duchesne-Guillemin (1948), all the specialists of the Old Avesta developed an essentially biographical interpretation of the text. The *Gāθās* were a personal work— that of a lifetime—by which the prophet Zarathustra preached a new doctrine to men. Later studies, however, above all those of Helmut Humbach on the *Gāθās* (1959) and that of Johanna Narten on the *Yasna Haptaŋhāiti* (1986), have proved conclusively that the Old Avesta can not be understood in such a manner. We are not dealing with sermons addressed to men, but with hymns to the gods, which in their rhetorics resemble the hymns of the *Rigveda* and were meant to accompany the stages of a sacrificial ceremony, of which, however, no complete or detailed description is given. The singer neither describes how the sacrifice proceeds, nor does he narrate the exploits of the gods. Instead he explains the spirit of the ritual to the gods. What we find in the Old Avesta is the answer to certain questions, nothing more: Why is the ritual what it is? To whom should it be addressed? How can we first bring it to the gods' attention, then make them understand it, and finally make it effective? What can the gods expect from it, and what can the humans expect from it in return?

Aša

I shall begin by answering the first and last questions, which are both, in fact, about the purpose of the sacrifice. The central notion of the Old Avestan system is that of ordered structure, Aša. This is the fundamental principle of the Mazdean cosmogony. Ahura Mazdā engendered it at the dawn of time, which makes it an abstraction that defines the ideal functioning of the universe, as well as a minor god, son of Ahura Mazdā. It is what is commonly called in the jargon of Mazdean studies an Entity. Aša is not opposed to its antonym, which would be "chaos," in the way its OInd. equivalent *ṛtá-* is opposed to *ánṛta-*, but rather to a principle referred to by the feminine noun *druj-*, approximately "deception," which is not the "disorder," but a bad order, a false or deceptive order. Ahura Mazdā, however, and the order that he engendered are inseparably connected with the light of day. The second and third chapters of the *Yasna Haptaŋhāiti* (Y.36-37) underline as clearly as one could wish their celestial-diurnal nature and the splendid beauty which makes them the object one wishes to see. Thus, the fundamental opposition between Aša and Druj is between the order of day which is real, certain, because it can be seen, and the indistinct, mystifying, and threatening order of the night.

By organizing the world according to the principle of order, Ahura Mazdā set in motion the great natural cycles which allow life to develop on the surface of the earth. But this work is never finished. On one hand, the primordial achievement must be magnified, for if not, the god might allow the work to be undone; on the other, the god must be aided in maintaining the permanent cohesion of the universe. This is the double task that falls to human piety, which is above all expressed in the ritual activity. The duty of the sacrificer is to pay homage to the gods by completing without fault a long, complete, and complicated ceremony. To complete this performance is to do what Ahura Mazdā did at the dawn of time: produce order. The men reproduce symbolically the cosmogonic act of Ahura Mazdā by submitting the sacrifice to a perfect order. Aša, like OInd. *ṛtá-*, is also a ritual allegory and even one of the possible names for the ritual, for the ritual is the foremost ordered human activity. Such is, then, the answer to the first question, why is the ritual what it is?—the ritual is what it is because its order is supposed to reproduce the cosmogony. And here we also have one of its purposes. The function of the order of the sacrifice is to revaccinate the order of the universe, which it glorifies and whose duration it magically ensures.

The sacrifice is not only commemoration and preservation; however, it has another purpose, as well, which does not look back to past order, but constitutes for each man a promise of a future. The supreme objective of the ritual is a recompense (*mīžda*), which we should in fact understand as eschatological recompense, that is, the ritual allows man to obtain paradise.

*The exchange of gifts (*maga-*), souls, and* daēnās

The sacrificial ceremony involves an exchange (*maga*) of movements and gifts and is therefore conceived on the model of a hospitality ritual. The men invite the gods who should be invited and receive them with offerings of welcome that strengthen their power and guarantee their immortality at the same time that they oblige the gods to reciprocate both here and now and in the future. The essence of these reciprocal gifts, whatever their material form, is therefore none other than life, health in its various aspects, and, finally, immortality. These life forces are conceived as the "spoils" (*āiiapta*) that it is the ritual's task to win.

From the men's point of view, offering the gods immortality implies that the sacrifice involves the offering of something regarded as immortal. This function is that of the soul" (*uruuan*) of the sacrificed cow, in which the entire eschatological symbolism is crystallized. It arrives in the divine world by the ritual road and is, in each ceremony, the substitute of the human *uruuan* and travels in anticipation the road that it will one day travel toward the beyond. Here it will reach the goal that every faithful has chosen by his ritual practices: the infinite lights and the tent of Ahura Mazdā or the "long darkness" and the tent of the Lie. The soul of the cow, however, is not alone on its journey. A specialized part of the soul of the sacrificer, the *daēnā*, is launched on the ritual road and accompanies the soul of the victim. By this motif the sacrifice constitutes a symbolic anticipation of death and the final journey into the beyond. Some strophes suggest that this funerary rehearsal was acted out physically by a simulated death, either by mime or as the effect of an induced ecstasy.

The gods show men their generosity on three distinct levels. Here and now, as perceptible and immediate counter-gift, it bestows upon "this state," "the bony state," that is, on the living bodies, health and the weaker, but rational, forms of immortality consisting in longevity and offspring. But health and immortality, the spoils won by "the state of thought," that of the ritual, are also promised to the man who, in the ritual or in death, is himself, too, reduced to "the state of thought." The reciprocity only takes place, in concrete and conclusive manner, on the future day when the soul and the body have separated. At that time the gods really return the hospitality that the sacrifices showed them. Every man who has performed correct rituals will be received by them. Until then, each sacrifice offered anticipates symbolically and actually the acquisition of the permanent life forces that are promised for the beyond. In this way, the ritual is the dress rehearsal of death, the journey toward the beyond, and the reception among the gods.

Time

With its double function, commemorative and looking ahead, the sacrifice is situated at a pivotal point in time. Between the past of the divine cosmogonic acts and the future of individual deaths, both areas to which in theory the human spirit has no access, it is a present that is renewed from ceremony to ceremony. This representation of time is the target of a conscious speculation. It must be a rhetorical feature that each great *Gāθā* (1-3) includes a relatively long questioning of the deity. This stage of the ritual, referred to by the technical term *frasā*, is in two parts. The first concerns the *paouruuīm* "the first, the initial." The second does not have an explicit objective, but it must be, for the sake of symmetry and complementarity, the *apəməm* "the last, the final." This structure is very clear in the *Uštauuaitī Gāθā*. The questioning starts in Y.44.2 by *kaθā ... paouruuīm* "How is the initial?" followed by a series of questions about the cosmogony (Y.44.3-7). Strophe 8 is obviously a transition, where the questioning is suspended for several verses, and the following questions are with regard to the journey of the *uruuan* and the *daēnā*, on the conquest of immortality, and the final reward (Y.44.9-18). In the *Ahunauuaitī* the scheme is the same, except that the questions about the *paouruuīm* are omitted because the singer prefers to present it as something he is perfectly certain about (Y.31.11-13). His questioning begins in the next strophe with the following program Y.31.14): *tā θβā pərəsā ... yā zī āitī jā̊ghaitcā* "I ask you about the things that are coming and those that will come." We see that, while showing his interest in the future, the singer introduces an important nuance in its analysis: the distinction between "that which is coming" and "that which will come," which can only be between the near future and the distant future. The structure of the questioning allows us to see relatively clearly what is meant by it. Strophes 14-17 are about the future course of the sacrifice in progress and its conclusion, while strophes 18-21 are about the fate of the individual soul, but in a different form from the questioning section. For the singer there is thus a cosmic time whose future is death of man and a ritual time whose future is the good or bad end of the sacrifice. In fact, if the sacrifice is the present, its duration is not zero. At the moment the singer speaks he has a past and a present. The duration of the world and that of the sacrifice are complementary. Before the *frasā*, the singer has already expressed his ritual preference, which consists in chasing away the demons and inviting the gods favorable to him. Next, he has uttered the opinion that, among these gods, Ahura Mazdā is the "most beneficent" of all the gods. The singer has based these two preliminary operations upon the knowledge he has of the cosmic past, and after this it is the future he intends to ponder.

Thus, the sacrifice is at the same time the present and a microcosmos of the duration of the universe. It is striking that this representation is molded after the structure of the verbal categories that express the various aspects of the present. The ceremony, once finished, is followed sooner or later by another: the sacrifice is iterative like the present injunctive. Each ceremony obeys a particular law regarding how long it is to last: the sacrifice is durative like the present indicative. The only moments without thickness are those in which the words of the singer coincide with the operation he is conducting. This is precisely the case when he says: "I ask you." The sacrifice is then performative, like the aorist injunctive.[2] It is not by chance that the moment of the *frasā* is the pivot of the ritual time.

---

2   See Hoffmann, 1967, p. 251 and n. 275.

The maniiu-

Being at the same time present and a miniaturized representation of duration, the sacrifice is the agent of the dualist causality. Through it the confrontation of the initial principles of Aṣa and the Druj has an implication, in real time, for the end of each individual and within its own time determines the final success or failure of the ritual. In the ritual, the cosmogony is tied up with the eschatology by allowing the antagonism Aṣa/Druj to occupy the entire duration. At the same time, it bestows on man the mental means to explore the duration. Man should and must have a first mental reaction, the *maniiu*, to the most inaccessible past. It is a kind of realization and awareness, preliminary and underlying the thought itself, which constitutes itself instantaneously, without any process of elaboration. It is obvious that Ahura Mazdā's cosmogonic act is beyond direct confirmation, and, yet, man must learn about it because he must make his ritual choice matching this act, which the *maniiu*, or his opinion about Mazdā, allows him to do. It is a kind of instrument for knowing the past. By giving man a certain idea about the cosmogony, it allows him to adjust his ritual accordingly. Here we may ask ourselves whether such a power or feeling also gives the sacrificer some idea about the future of his sacrifice or that of his soul. Here things are quite clear, although less explicit, for this feeling is well attested in the Indo-Iranian tradition. I believe this is the role of the *zarazdā-*, that is, "faith," the feeling that enables the sacrificer who has completed the ritual appropriately to be intimately convinced that the divinity can not let him down.

Seeing and hearing: communication

The sacrifice is the place and time where gods and men meet. Just as men must express to the gods what their opinion is and bring the sacrifice to their attention, so too must the gods convey to men their ritual demands. Thus, communication is essential. For Old Avestan man the communication takes place through the complementarity of seeing and hearing. The ritual demands that gods and men make themselves heard and seen, exchange words and visible signs. For that, man has at his disposal the word (*vacah-*, *uxδa-*) and the action (*šiiaoθana-*), that is, the sum of liturgical recitations and actions. As for the gods, on one hand, the light of day is their visible and marvelous form, and, on the other, they transmit to men the precise words through which they express their will: the archetypal plan (*ratu-*), the formula (*mąθra-*), the teaching (*sāsnā-*), the precept (*sāx^van-*), and the condition of alliance (*uruuata-*).

By the magic of the ritual, all the moments of the cosmic duration become accessible to the sight and hearing (without taking precedence over the *maniiu*, which presupposes the other two). The great divine acts of the past can be the object of poetic or mystic vision (thus, Y.45.8 "I have just seen with my own eye ... that Ahura Mazdā is (the one who planted the pickets of the [cosmic] structure)"). The poem fixes the memory of it and perpetuates this fame or this reputation, which is also its own name (*srauuah-*). In the same way, the complementarity of seeing and hearing has an important place in the representations of after-life. We have seen that the ritual and death launch the wandering soul (*daēnā-*) on the road into the beyond. This soul is not only defined by its name as ability to see, but also has an intimate and multilateral relationship that is active, passive, and causative, with the act of seeing, which is expressed by the verb *cit* "to notice." The *daēnā* is seen, sees, and causes to see. It is the only thing that the *uruuan* that has left the body sees of the world around it. It performs the function assumed in India by the king of the dead, Yama, which is to see the road and show it to the *uruuan*, which she guides. Having taken on the form of a beautiful young woman or of a horrible old one, by her remarkable beauty or ugliness she immediately reveals to the gods the merit or lack of merit of the one she is guiding to them, as well as his quality of being a follower of Aṣa or of the Druj. The hearing ability also plays a clear, though covert, role. The Young Avesta contains the motif of the horn of Yima, which synchronically no longer has anything to do with death but, by occupying an intermediate position between the flute of Yama and the trumpet of doom, allows us hypothetically to reconstruct the complementarity of seeing and hearing of the original myth. I am inclined to believe that the Indo-Iranian dead possessed an ability of seeing that allowed them to follow the road into the beyond and that the king of the dead, without necessarily leaving his domain, either lent their journeying assistance by producing some kind of sound or had sent them a musical invitation to die.

Men and gods must also have a mutual inclination to see and hear one another. This requirement is particularly clear in the case of hearing. The benevolent readiness to listen, *sraoša*, refers both to the merciful attention of the gods and man's will to obey. In the Young Avesta it was to become an entity and even a divinity in its own right. It is not by chance that it plays an essential role in the reception committee to enter paradise. The good readiness to see is not clearly attested, but we know that it played a role in the Indo-Iranian tradition (the Vedic *vená-*), and it seems to be represented in the Old Avesta in various forms of "scouting," expressed by words such as *išti* and *vaēda*, although these operations are not necessarily performed by sight.

Thought

Yet it is also clear that the word, the action, hearing, and sight are not all and do not play a primary role in the relationship between gods and men. The word and the action are only the extension, the material manifestation of a fundamental force, both within and beyond discernible perception, namely, thought. In the Old Avestan analysis, a living being is characterized by having a body. Its mode of existence is the "osseous state," the "state of bones," which manifests certain subtle powers not shared by matter or plants, such as the sense of perception (*baodah-*) and free movement (*uštāna-*). An additional feature of man is that when he sacrifices he leaves this state and enters the "state of thought"—typical of the gods—which makes him worthy and capable of obtaining contact with the gods. That is why this state of thought is called first, primordial, important. It causes the greatness of the gods and constitutes human nature. It is also the state to which man is reduced after death when he becomes the guest of the gods. Its special importance is clearly revealed by the fact that the two entities that together with Aša constitute the minor pantheon of Mazdaism are not only ritual allegories but also allegories of thought: Vohu Manah, Good Thought, et Ārmaiti, Docility. Ārmaiti, which is the mental submission to the divine demands and ordinances, functions exclusively in the strict framework of the ritual as relationship principle between men and gods. Vohu Manah, which is both good and divine thought, ensures the connection between the ritual behavior and the principle of ordered cosmic structure. It is the faculty that allows man to recognize this structure, to understand it, and to reproduce it in his behavior, in a perception which puts him in harmony with the god and, in some way, on his level: "to think ordered structure" is both the archetypal act of Ahura Mazdā and the characteristic feature of the good sacrificer.

The fire

We understand that this kind of information exchange between men and gods is not automatic. How could a man be certain that the god is inclined to hear and see him? How can he, materially, hear the divine words? How can he know if the great light which comes from the celestial space acquires here and now a special and attentive presence? The communication can not take place without a transmission mechanism. This function of specialized agent, of the ritual go-between, is performed by the fire, who is the supreme instrument of the ritual. It is the pivot of the sacrifice, the point of convergence of all the symbols he puts into play. It owes this role not only to its mystical essence, but also to the fact that he is regarded both as a god and as a sacrificer, that is, as an entity that incorporates the two interlocutors of the sacrifice and therefore is characterized by precious ambivalences. While the sacrifice reproduces symbolically a scene of hospitality, the fire, center of the family, is the primary comfort offered to the guest, and as a god living among men, he is himself the primary guest (*asti-*). The crackling and the light are complementary signals of the words and actions of the men: he makes the sacrifice heard and seen, and he is its messenger (*dūta-*). His subtle and magical nature even allows him to be identified with the *maniiu* (Y.36.3). The fire is the visible manifestation of men's opinion about Ahura Mazdā, and he reveals directly to the gods the most secret and most elementary of human behaviors. To light a fire in the right place and at the right moment, to gather around it, to declare solemnly that he is the representative of the great divine light, means that one has the good opinion about Ahura Mazdā. In return, the fire seizes the divine signals. He hears the formulas (*mąθrān-*) and materializes in a delimited body, at the heart of the ceremony, this light that is the visible form of the gods. As admirably discerned by Johanna Narten, the consecration of the ritual fire consists of affirming the transsubstantiation that turns a banal fire, lit by the hand of man, into a spark of the great celestial fire (Y.36). As such, the fire is he who reveals the ordered structure and so becomes the primary "support of the structured order" (*aṣauuan-*) and thereby participates in the nature of Ahura Mazdā: he is "like you, (Mazdā)" (*θβāuuaṇt-*), and he is also, like Mazdā, the master (*ahura-*). Its immobility, which is at paradoxical variance with the rise of the smoke and the light toward the sky, is like that of the perfect sacrificer, who stands impeccably still, unmoving and even rigid, in an position that affirms a striking particularity of the human species and probably symbolizes the axis mundi. And yet, as we have seen, one of the specialized faculties of the sacrificer, the *daēnā*, must leave him to go to the gods. By its ascending movement toward heaven, the fire shows that he knows how to perform this journey. Going from the men toward the gods, he is for the latter the conveyer who brings them the offerings (*vāzišta*) and for the former he who teaches the road leading to the dwellings of the gods and to the beyond (*āsīšti-*).

The gods

In the same way that there is a good and an evil cosmic principle, a good and an evil resting-place for the dead, good and bad sacrificers, so also are there good and bad deities, that is, deities who take sides for Aṣa or for the Druj. The Gathic sacrificer must know how to distinguish between them and so choose his camp. This operation takes place once in every *Gāθā*, which means that it is a necessary and important stage of the ritual, at the juncture of ceremonial time. The singer ceases his direct invocation of Ahura Mazdā and addresses a multiplicity of gods, whom he calls either "(you) who are" (*haṇt-*, pres. part. of *ah-* "to be") or "(you) who wish to come" (*išəṇt-*, pres. part. of the desiderative of *i-* "to go, come"). The latter are thus those who are hurrying toward the sacrificial ground. Among these deities, all eager to collect the offerings, the sacrificer must select by solemn proclamation those that he excludes (*var: vāurua-*) and those that he invites (*zū: zbaiia-*). The act of distinguishing and choosing certain gods who are then rejected and others who are received hospitably has the technical name *āuuarəna-*, that is, "declaration of ritual preference." To a certain extent, this declaration continues a traditional Indo-Iranian practice, for it is in principle analogous to the *ādeśa-* of the *Brāhmaṇa*s, which is the official notification that the sacrifice is being rendered to such a god rather than another. Nevertheless, there is a considerable difference between the two. The aim is not to make known to which specific god the sacrifice will be rendered, but to make a fundamental sectioning of the collection of gods. The *Gāθās* pronounce a negative judgment, even condemn most strongly and in the most insulting fashion the gods who are to be turned away. It is not about selecting in the positive pantheon this or that deity, but—no more and no less—saying which are the gods and which are the demons. From this point of view, the *āuuarəna-* corresponds less to the ritual roll-call than to the preliminary precaution that consists in undertaking nothing with respect to the gods before having proclaimed the exclusion of the *asura* and the *rakṣas*. The ritual selection consists of taking the consequences of the effect on the pantheon of the Aša/Druj antagonism. According to the Gathic dualism, practicing a good ritual is impossible without at the same time execrating the bad one, those to whom the latter is addressed, and those who practice it (be they imaginary). The role of victims of the ritual selection is played by the *daēuuas*. These are essentially this cursed part of the pantheon that deserves no sacrifice and whose exclusion accompanies the invitation sent to the good deities. They appear, only to be chased away, which is what happens to demons.

Since the Iranian *daēuuas/daivas* have never been anything but demons, where did the gods of the Indo-Iranian pantheon go to in the Old Avesta? Some heavy-weight scholars, like Mary Boyce, think we should not let ourselves be deceived by the absence of their names and that at least some of them nonetheless belong to the religious system.[3] The debate over the ritual that we see being played out in the Old Avesta could very well in part be this: on what should one base the ranking of Ahura Mazdā as the primary target of the sacrifice and what residual share should be reserved for the gods of the traditional pantheon? The answer to the first part of the question is clear: the sacrifice must first and foremost be addressed to Ahura Mazdā because it is he who makes the sacrifice yield maximum dividend. The preeminence of Ahura Mazdā and the subordinate function of the gods thus becomes perfectly clear. Mazdā is the originator of the cosmogony and master of the resting-place of the dead, which is his dwelling, while the gods protect the orderly functioning of the various departments of the

---

3   Boyce, 1969, pp. 10-34.

universe and stand guard, as it were, at the entrance of the beyond. In the same way, Ahura Mazdā is the preferred and nominal target of the sacrifice, which does not mean, however, that the other gods are denied or excluded from the ceremony. A discrete part of the sacrifice may have been conceded to them, by anonymous, but benevolent, association with the invocation of the great god. The privilege granted the latter and denied the former is the uttering of the name, which becomes the precise sign and characteristic of the hierarchy of the pantheon. It is certain that this particularity of the Old Avestan Mazdaism did not last for long. For there is a clear polemical intention in the manner in which the *yašts* affirm the sacrificial dignity of the gods, either by conferring on them the title of *yazata* "worthy of sacrifice," or by enumerating as models to be followed the sacrificers of the mythical past. It is the same kind of idea that underlies the harsh demand of the gods Miθra and Tištriia upon their worshipper that he should sacrifice to them "mentioning the name." It is as if the gods of the Young Avesta, without disputing the supremacy of Ahura Mazdā, were reclaiming a nominal ritual independence that had been confiscated from them.

The two states of existence

The ideology of the ritual described above is thus characterized by a speculation consisting in establishing degrees of existence. The totality of the ordered world is characterized by existence, being (*sti-*). The particularity of living beings is to have a "bony state" (*ahu- astuuaṇt-*), and among these men and gods have one privilege in common, namely, the "state of thought" (*ahu- manax̌iia-*). The two states are combined in living man, whose "life" (*gaiia-*) can be defined as thought as manifested in the physical realities of word and action. The state of thought is thus reduced to itself in the case of man when dead and the gods. The difference between men and gods lies in their position with respect to time, which means that the speculation about existence is finally combined with that about time, which we have already spoken about. The gods as a totality, good or bad, are referred to by a form of the verb "to be," either the present participle "those being" or by the relative clause "who are [present indicative]" or in expanded form, "those who have been [perfect], those who are, and those who shall be [aorist subjunctive]." It is the last expression that reveals the explicit meaning of the designation, the other two being merely elliptical variants of the last. We must not, however, see in the use of the verb "to be" in Indo-Iranian a peremptory affirmation of existence, but rather the realization of this permanence that is the primordial characteristic of the gods. Men, defined by their name as "mortal" (*marəta-*, *maṣ̌iia-*, *maṣ̌iiāka-*), are necessarily those "who have been, who are" or "who shall be." By contrast, the gods are living beings whose existence stretches out without restriction over past, present, and future, thus merging, if not with eternity, at least with the duration of the cosmos. Nevertheless, the divine categories are unequal from the point of view of time, which is another aspect of the divine hierarchy. The Entities, engendered by Ahura Mazdā, had a beginning, but will have no end. For this reason they will be, at some moment or other, partially defined by their specific title as "immortal" (*aməṣ̌a-*). The only title the traditional gods have in the Old Avesta is the one which refers to their permanent existence (see above). Indeed, in the Young Avesta they appear as essentially preoccupied with ensuring the reproduction and the regularity of the natural cycles which constitute time, with which their existence is fused: the alternation of day and night, the sequence of seasons, the rotation of the stars, human recurrent phenomena (menses, pregnancies, meals, waking and sleep). Their field of action is the entire duration of the cosmos. Ahura Mazdā, however, is one up on them, for he transcends time.[4] By engaging the mechanism of the succession of the dawns, he started the course of time. He rules over the resting-place of the dead, where the unending lights do not alternate with any night. For every deceased, his own *daēnā* is felt to be an interior, definitive, dawn, which abolishes time. Thus, Ahura Mazdā is both the originator of time and the god whose dwelling is situated outside time.

As we see, the Old Avestan ritual is a speculative ritual, which on no account contains the Mazdean philosophy, but opens up the path along which it will proceed in the distant future.

---

4   It is possible that the title of *ahura* implies a certain relationship with existence, not by etymology (Mayrhofer, 1992, pp. 147-148), but by etymological speculation.

ABBREVIATIONS

Aog.	*Aogəmadaēca* (ed. Jamaspasa)
Her.	*Hērbedestān* (ed. Humbach-Elfenbein, Kotwal-Kreyenbroek)
Nir.	*Nīrangestān* (ed. Sanjana)
OAv.	Old Avestan
Purs.	*Pursišnīhā* (ed. JamaspAsa-Humbach)
RV.	R̥gveda
V.	Videvdad (*Widēwdād*, Vendidad)
Vr.	*Vispered*
Y.	*Yasna*
YAv.	Young Avestan
Yt.	*Yašt*

AoF	*Altorientalische Forschungen*
BSL	*Bulletin de la Société Linguistique de Paris*
BSOAS	*Bulletin of the School of Oriental and African Studies*
CRAI	*Comptes-rendus de l'Académie des Inscriptions et Belles-Lettres*
IIJ	*Indo-Iranian Journal*
JA	*Journal Asiatique*
JNES	*Journal of Near Eastern Studies*
JRAS	*Journal of the Royal Asiatic Society*
MSS	*Münchener Studien zur Sprachwissenschaft*
NGWG	*Nachrichten von der königlichen Gesellschaft der Wissenschaften zu Göttingen*
OLZ	*Orientalistische Literaturzeitung*
ZDMG	*Zeitschrift der Deutschen Morgenländischen Gesellschaft*

BIBLIOGRAPHY

Andreas, F. C., "Die Entstehung des Awesta-Alphabets und sein ursprünglicher Lautwert," in *Verhandlungen des XIII. Internationalen Orientalisten-Kongresses. Hamburg, September 1902*, Leiden, 1904, pp. 99-106.

Andreas, F. C., "Die dritte Ghāthā des Zura^xthušthro (Josno 30)," *NGWG*, phil.-hist. Kl., 1909, pp. 42-49.

Andreas, F. C., and J. Wackernagel, "Die vierte Ghāthā des Zura^Xthušthro (Josno 31)," *NGWG*, phil.-hist. Kl., 1911, pp. 1-34.

Andreas, F. C., and J. Wackernagel, "Die erste, zweite und fünfte Ghāthā des Zura^xthušthro (Josno 28. 29. 32). Versuch einer Herstellung der älteren Textformen nebst Übersetzung," *NGWG*, phil.-hist. Kl., 1913, pp. 363-85.

Andreas, F. C., and J. Wackernagel, "Die erste, zweite und fünfte Ghāthā des Zurathušthro (Josno 28. 29. 32). Anmerkungen," *NGWG*, phil.-hist. Kl., 1931, pp. 304-29.

Anquetil-Duperron, A. H., *Zend-Avesta. Ouvrage de Zoroastre*, Paris, 1771.

Bailey, H. W., review of J. Duchesne-Guillemin, *Les composés de l'Avesta*, Liège and Paris, 1936, in *JRAS*, 1939, pp. 112-117.

Bailey, H. W., *Zoroastrian Problems in the Ninth-Century Books*, Oxford, 1943; 2nd ed. with new introduction, London, 1971.

Bartholomae, C., *Arische Forschungen* I, Halle, 1882.

Bartholomae, C., "Vorgeschichte der Iranischen Sprachen" and "Awestasprache und Altpersisch," in W. Geiger and E. Kuhn, *Grundriss der Iranischen Philologie*, Strassburg, 1895-1901, repr. Berlin and New York, 1974.

Bartholomae, C., *Altiranisches Wörterbuch*, Strassburg, 1904; repr. Berlin, 1961.

Bartholomae, C., *Die Gatha's des Awesta. Zarathustra's Verspredigten*, Strassburg, 1905.

Bartholomae, C., *Zum Altiranischen Wörterbuch*, Strassburg, 1906.

Bartholomae, C., *Zarathuštra's Leben und Lehre. Akademische Rede (Heidelberg 22. November 1918)*, Kultur und Sprache 4, Heidelberg,

1924; repr. in *Zarathustra*, ed. B. Schlerath, Darmstadt: Wissenschaftliche Buchgesellschaft, 1970.

Baunack, Th., *Studien auf dem Gebiete der griechischen und arischen Sprachen I/II: Der Yasna Haptaŋhāiti*, Leipzig, 1888.

Beekes, R. S. P., *A Grammar of Gatha-Avestan*, Leiden, etc., 1988.

Benveniste, E., *The Persian Religion According to the Chief Greek Texts*, Paris, 1929.

Benveniste, E., "Les classes sociales dans la tradition avestique," *JA*, 1932, pp. 117-134.

Benveniste, E., "Le système phonologique de l'iranien ancien," *BSL* 62, 1968, pp. 53-64.

Boyce, M., "On Mithra's Part in Zoroastrianism," *BSOAS* 32, 1969, pp. 10-34.

Boyce, M., "On the Antiquity of Zoroastrian Apocalyptic," *BSOAS* 47, 1984, pp. 57-75.

Boyce, M., *A History of Zoroastrianism*, Handbuch der Orientalistik I, viii: Religion 1, 2, 2A, Leiden and Cologne; I. *The Early Period*, 1975; II. *Under the Achaemenians*, 1982.

Boyce, M., *Zoroastrianism*, Costa Mesa, 1992.

Carnoy, A., "Le nom des Mages," *Le Muséon*, 1908, pp. 121-158.

Christol, A., "De ΦΟΩΣ 'ΕΡΕΩΝ à *ā dyām tanoṣi*. Note de phraséologie," *BSL* 81, 1986, pp. 181-204.

Christol, A., "Les huttes cosmiques. Pour une archéologie formulaire du Véda," *Bulletin des Études Indiennes* 5, 1987, pp. 11-36.

Darmesteter, J., *Le Zend-Avesta*, 3 vols., Annales du Musée Guimet 21-24, Paris, 1892-3; repr. Paris, 1960.

Duchesne-Guillemin, J., "La religion des Achéménides," *Historia* 18, 1972, pp. 59-82 (= *Opera Minora* I, Tehran, 1974, pp. 66-90).

Duchesne-Guillemin, "Le dieu de Cyrus," in *Commémoration Cyrus. Actes du congrès de Shiraz 1971 ... Hommage Universel* II, Acta Iranica 3, Tehran and Liège, 1975, pp. 11-21 (= *Opera Minora* II, pp. 367-377).

Duchesne-Guillemin, J., *Zoroastre. Étude critique avec une traduction commentée des Gâthâ*, Paris, 1948.

Duchesne-Guillemin, J., *The Hymns of Zarathustra*, tr. M. Henning, London, 1952.

Dumézil, G., *Naissance d'Archanges. Essai sur la formation de la théologie mazdéenne*, Paris, 1945.

Dumézil, G., "A propos de la plainte de l'âme du bœuf (Yasna 29),"
    Bulletin de l'Académie royale de Belgique 51, 1965, pp. 23-51.

Dumézil, G., *Les Dieux souverains des Indo-européens*, Paris, 1977.

Fussman, G., "Problématique des religions indiennes anciennes," *JA* 265,
    1977, pp. 21-68.

Geldner, K.F., *Drei Yasht aus dem Zendavesta*, Stuttgart, 1884.

Geldner, K.F., "Yasna 46," *Beiträge zur Kunde der indogermanischen
    Sprachen* 14, Göttingen, 1889, pp. 1-28.

Geldner, K. F., *Avesta, the Sacred Book of the Parsis*, 3 vols., Stuttgart,
    1896.

Gershevitch, I., review of Humbach, 1959, in *BSOAS* 25, 1962, pp. 367-
    370.

Gershevitch, I., *The Avestan Hymn to Mithra*, Cambridge, 1959.

Gershevitch, I., "Zoroaster's Own Contribution," *JNES* 23, 1964, pp. 12-38.

Gignoux, Ph., "Corps osseux et âme osseuse," *JA* 267, 1979, pp. 41-79.

Gignoux, Ph., "Nouveaux regards sur l'apocalypse iranienne," *CRAI*, 1986,
    pp. 334-346.

Gnoli, G., *Zoroaster's Time and Homeland*, Naples, 1980.

Henning, W. B., *Zoroaster. Politician or Witch-Doctor*, London, 1951.

Herrenschmidt, C., "Notes sur la parenté chez les perses au début de
    l'empire achéménide," in H. Sancisi-Weerdenburg and A. Kuhrt,
    eds., *Achaemenid History* II: *The Greek Sources*, Leiden, 1987, pp.
    53-67.

Hertel, J., *Die arische Feuerlehre*, Leipzig, 1925.

Herzfeld, E., *Zoroaster and His World*, Princeton, 1947.

Hoffmann, K., *Der Injunktiv im Veda*, Heidelberg, 1967.

Hoffmann, K., *Aufsätze zur Indoiranistik*, 2 vols., Wiesbaden, 1975.

Humbach, H., "Gast und Gabe bei Zarathustra," *MSS* 2, 1952, pp. 5-34.

Humbach, "Rituelle Termini technici in den awestischen Gathas," *MSS* 8,
    1956, pp. 74-83.

Humbach, H., *Die Gathas des Zarathustra*, 2 vols., Heidelberg, 1959.

Humbach, H., "Neue chwaresmologische Arbeiten," *ZDMG* 123, 1973, pp.
    83-97.

Humbach, H., "Zarathustra und die Rinderschlachtung," in *Wort und
    Wirklichkeit. Studien zur Afrikanistik und Orientalistik Eugen
    Ludwig Rapp zum 70. Geburtstag* II: *Linguistik und Kulturwissen-
    schaft*, Meisenheim am Glan, 1977, pp. 17-29.

Humbach, H., and J. Elfenbein, *Ērbedestān. An Avesta-Pahlavi Text*, Munich, 1990.

JamaspAsa, K. M., *Aogəmadaēcā. A Zoroastrian Liturgy*, Vienna, 1982.

JamaspAsa, K. M., and H. Humbach, *Pursišnīhā. A Zoroastrian Catechism*, 2 vols., Wiesbaden, 1971.

Insler, S., *The Gāthās of Zarathustra*, Acta Iranica 8, Tehran and Liège, 1975.

Kellens, J., see the complete bibliography below.

Klein, J., *Toward a Discourse Grammar of the Rigveda*, 2 vols., Heidelberg, 1985.

Kotwal, F. M., and Kreyenbroek, Ph. G., *The Hērbedestān and Nērangestān*, Paris. Vol. I: *Hērbedestān*, 1992. Vol. II: *Nērangestān, Fragard 1*, 1995.

Kreyenbroek, G., *Sraoša in the Zoroastrian Tradition*, Leiden, 1985.

Kuiper, F. B. J. "Avestan *mazdā*," *IIJ* 1, 1957, pp. 86-95.

Kuiper, F.B. J., "The Ancient Aryan Verbal Contest," *IIJ* 4, 1960, pp. 217-281.

Lommel, H., ed. B. Schlerath, *Die Gathas des Zarathustra*, Basel, 1971.

Mayrhofer, M., *Etymologisches Wörterbuch des Altindischen* I, Heidelberg, 1992.

Meillet, A., *Trois conférences sur les Gâthâ de l'Avesta*, Paris, 1925.

Molé, M., *Culte, mythe et cosmologie dans l'Iran ancien*, Paris, 1963.

Monna, M.C., *The Gathas of Zarathustra*, Leiden, 1978.

Narten, J., *Die Aməša Spəntas im Avesta*, Wiesbaden, 1982.

Narten, J., *Yasna Haptaŋhāiti*, Wiesbaden, 1986.

Nyberg, H. S., *Irans forntida religioner*, Stockholm, 1937.

Pirart, E., see the complete bibliography of Kellens, below.

Sanjana, D. P., *Nirangistan. A Photozincographed Facsimile*, Bombay, 1895.

Schlerath, B., review of Humbach, 1959, in *OLZ* 57, 1962, pp. 566-589.

Schmidt, H.P., "Die Komposition von Yasna 49," in *Pratidānam. Indo-Iranian Studies Presented to F.B.J. Kuiper on His Sixtieth Birthday*, The Hague and Paris, 1968, pp. 170-192.

Schmidt, H.-P., with contribs. of W. Lentz and S. Insler, *Form and Meaning of Yasna 33*, New Haven, 1985.

Schwijzer, E., "Die sog. mißbräuchlichen Instrumentale im Awesta," *Indogermanische Forschungen* 19, 1929, pp. 214-271.

Shaked, S., *Dualism in Transformation*, London, 1994.

Skjærvø, P. O., review of J. Narten, *Die Aməša Spəṇtas im Avesta*, Wiesbaden 1982, in *Kratylos* 28, 1983 [1984], pp. 77-81.

Skjærvø, P. O., "Zarathustra in the Avesta and in Manicheism. Irano-Manichaica III," in *La Persia e l'Asia centrale da Alessandro al X secolo* ... (Roma, 9-12 novembre 1994), Roma, 1996 [1997], pp. 597-628.

Skjærvø, P. O., "The Literature of the Most Ancient Iranians," in S. J. H. Manekshaw and P. R. Ichaporia, eds., *Proceedings of the Second North American Gatha Conference. Houston, Texas, 1996*, The Journal of the Research and Historical Preservation Committee 2, 1996 [1997], pp. 221-235.

Smith, M. W., *Studies in the Syntax of the Gathas of Zarathustra together with Text, Translation, and Notes*, Philadelphia, 1929, repr. New York, 1966.

Sundermann, W., "Die vierzehn Wunden der Lebendigen Seele," *AoF* 12, 1985, pp. 288-295.

BIBLIOGRAPHY OF THE WORKS OF JEAN KELLENS

1965

1 "Dans la pénombre sans mémoire où les genoux ...," in J. De Caluwé, ed., *Hommage à M. Robert Vivier*, Liège, 1965, pp. 155-161.

2 "Tracé par l'oubli," in J. De Caluwé, ed., *Hommage à M. Robert Vivier*, Liège 1965, pp. 177-180.

1966

3 *Le sentiment du moi dans la poésie de Jules Supervielle,* Ph.D. thesis, Liège, 1966.

1968

4 With Michel Defourny, *L'épisode de Sâvitrî ou Célébration de la fidélité*, Robert Morel: n.p., 1968.

1969

5 With Michel Defourny, *Le Dit du Poisson*, Guy Lévis-Mano: Paris, 1969.

6 *Quelques inscriptions de Darius et de Xerxès, L'Athénée*, 1969, pp. 77-85.

7 Review of *Studia et Acta Orientalia* V-VI, Bucarest, 1967, in *Marche Romane* 19, 1969, pp. 154-155.

8 "Sur un parallèle inverse à l'inscription des 'daivas'," *Studi e Materiali di Storia delle Religioni* 40, Rome, 1969, pp. 209-213.

1970

9 With M. Defourny, "Fables indiennes," *Revue des Langues vivantes* 36, 1970, pp. 412-420.

10 "Note sur un emploi du datif dans le 'Hom Yašt'," *Die Sprache* 16, 1970, pp. 78-79.

1971

11   Review of *Saeculum Weltgeschichte* I-II, in *Erasmus* 23, 1971, cols. 314-318.

1973

12   "L'avestique de 1962 à 1972," *Kratylos* 16, 1971 [1973], pp. 1-30.
13   "Les frauuašis dans l'art sassanide," *Iranica Antiqua* 10, 1973, pp. 133-138.

1974

14   "L'avestique de 1962 à 1972: addenda et corrigenda," *Kratylos* 18, 1973 [1974], pp. 1-5.
15   "'Prestige' et 'satisfaction' dans l'Avesta," *MSS* 32, 1974, pp. 87-101.
16   Review of *Saeculum Weltgeschichte* VI, in *Erasmus* 26, 1974, cols. 440-443.
17   "Les noms-racines avestiques," *BSL* 64, 1974, pp. 85-97.
18   *Les noms-racines de l'Avesta*, Wiesbaden, 1974.
19   "Saošiiaṇt," *Studia Iranica* 3, 1974, pp. 187-209.
20   "Xerxès, roi des rois," in *Commémoration Cyrus. Actes du congrès de Shiraz 1971 ... Hommage Universel* I, Acta Iranica 1, Tehran and Liège, 1974, pp. 108-116 (translation of M. Mayrhofer, *Xerxes, König der Könige*, Almanach der Österreichischen Akademie der Wissenschaften 119, Vienna, 1969, pp. 158-170).
21   "Iran et Tibet," in *Commémoration Cyrus. Actes du congrès de Shiraz 1971 ... Hommage Universel* I, Acta Iranica 1, Tehran and Liège, 1974, pp. 299-306 (translation of G. Tucci, "Iran e Tibet," in *La Persia nel medioevo*, Rome, 1971, pp. 355-360).
22   "Indo-Iranica," in *Commémoration Cyrus. Actes du congrès de Shiraz 1971 ... Hommage Universel* II, Acta Iranica 2, Tehran and Liège, 1974, pp. 63-90 (translation of G. Liebert, "Indo-Iranica: 1. a.-p. *vazraka-*, av. *vazra-*, a.-ind. *vájra-*," *Orientalia Suecana* 11, Stockholm, 1962, pp. 126-154).

23   "Les espions de Varuṇa et de Mitra et l'œil du roi," in *Commé-moration Cyrus. Actes du congrès de Shiraz 1971 ... Hommage Universel* II, Acta Iranica 2, Tehran and Liège, 1974, pp. 91-100 (translation of H. Lommel, "Die Späher des Varuṇa und Mitra und das Auge des Königs," *Oriens* 6, Ankara, 1953, pp. 323-333).

24   "Le caviar, étude lexicale," in *Commémoration Cyrus. Actes du congrès de Shiraz 1971 ... Hommage Universel* II, Acta Iranica 2, Tehran and Liège, 1974, pp. 381-390 (translation of W. Eilers, "Kaviar, eine Wortstudie," in C. Vogel, ed., *Jñānamuktāvalī. Commemoration Volume in Honour of Johannes Nobel*, New Delhi, 1963, pp. 48-58).

25   "Les relations entre le Portugal et la Perse," in *Commémoration Cyrus. Actes du congrès de Shiraz 1971 ... Hommage Universel* II, Acta Iranica 3, Tehran and Liège, 1974, pp. 411-417 (translation of L. De Matos, "Das relações entre Portugal e a Persia 1500-1758, in *Catálogo bibliográfico da exposição comemorativa de XXV centenário da Monarquia na Irão, organizada pela Fundacão Calouste Gulbenkian*, Lisbon, 1972, pp. 1-9).

26   "Le type *hubərəta- bar* en avestique," in *Commémoration Cyrus. Actes du congrès de Shiraz 1971 ... Hommage Universel* II, Acta Iranica 3, Tehran and Liège, 1974, pp. 133-147.

27   "Un nouveau trait du vocabulaire daevique," in *Commémoration Cyrus. Actes du congrès de Shiraz 1971 ... Hommage Universel* II, Acta Iranica 3, Tehran and Liège, 1974, pp. 149-156.

1975

28   *Fravardīn Yašt (Yt 13, 1-70),* Wiesbaden, 1975.

29   "Sur la transmission des Yašts," *MSS* 33, 1975, pp. 61-66.

30   "Mythes et conceptions avestiques sous les sassanides," in *Monumentum H.S. Nyberg* I, Acta Iranica 4, Tehran and Liège, 1975, pp. 457-470.

31   "L'expression avestique de la perpétuité," *IIJ* 17, 1975, 211-215.

32   "Yasna 31, 9: la faveur d'Ārmaiti," *Studia Iranica* 4, 1975, pp. 145-158.

1976

33   "Une correction au texte de l'Avesta," in *Miscellanea in Honorem Ibrahim Purdavud*, Farhang-e Iran Zamin 21, Tehran, 1976, pp. 73-78.

34   "Un prétendu présent radical," *MSS* 34, 1976, pp. 59-71.

35   "Trois réflexions sur la religion des Achéménides," *Studien zur Indologie und Iranistik* 2, Hamburg, 1976, pp. 113-132.

36   "Compléments sur le Yasna 31, 9," *Studia Iranica* 5, 1976, pp. 295-297.

37   "L'Avesta comme source historique: la liste des kayanides," in *Acta Antiqua Hungarica* 24, 1976, pp. 37-49.

38   "Un 'ghost-god' dans la tradition zoroastrienne," *IIJ* 18, 1976, pp. 89-95.

39   "Les présents avestiques *isa-* et *iša-*," *Zeitschrift für vergleichende Sprachwissenschaft* 90, 1976, pp. 87-103.

1977

40   "Vibration and Twinkling," *Journal of Indo-European Studies* 5, Washington, 1977, pp. 197-201.

41   "Une représentation trifonctionnelle de l'adolescence," *MSS* 36, 1977, pp. 53-57.

42   "Deuxième colloque sur l'histoire de l'Asie Centrale préislamique," in *Onoma* 21, 1977, pp. 597-598.

43   Review of M. Mayrhofer, *Zum Namengut des Avesta*, Vienna, 1977, in *Onoma* 21, 1977, pp. 662-667.

1978

44   "Caractères différentiels du Mihr Yašt," in *Études Mithriaques*, Acta Iranica 17, Tehran and Liège, 1978, pp. 261-270.

45   Review of K. Mylius, *Wörterbuch Sanskrit-Deutsch*, Leipzig, 1975, in *L'Antiquité Classique* 47, Bruxelles, 1978, pp. 302-303.

1979

46   "Les bras de Mithra," in U. Bianchi, ed., *Mysteria Mithrae*, Rome and Leiden, 1979, pp. 703-716.

47   Review of M. Mayrhofer, *Die avestischen Namen*, Vienna, 1977, in *Onoma* 23, 1979, pp. 186-189.

48   Review of M. Mayrhofer, *Nachlese altpersischer Inschriften*, Innsbruck, 1978, and *Supplement zur Sammlung der altpersischen Inschriften*, Vienna, 1978, in *Onoma* 23, 1979, pp. 189-192.

49   Review of R. Schmitt, *Die Iranier-Namen bei Aischylos*, Vienna, 1978, in *Onoma* 23, 1979, pp. 192-193.

50   Review of J. Haudry, *L'emploi des cas en védique*, Lyon, 1977, in *ZDMG* 129, 1979, p. 426.

51   "Remarques sur le Fravardīn Yašt," *Acta Antiqua Academiae Scientiarum Hungaricae* 25 (*Festschrift János Harmatta*), 1977, pp. 69-73.

1980

52   "La prière d'identification dans la tradition zoroastrienne," in H. Limet and J. Ries, eds., *L'expérience de la prière dans les grandes religions: actes du colloque de Louvain-la-Neuve et Liège (22-23 novembre 1978)*, Louvain, 1980, pp. 119-128.

53   "Avestique *auua-θβars*," *MSS* 39, 1980, pp. 59-61.

54   Review of K. Mylius, *Älteste indische Dichtung und Prosa*, Leipzig, 1978, in *L'Antiquité Classique* 49, 1980, pp. 455-456.

55   Review of K. Mylius, *Chrestomathie der Sanskrit-literatur*, Leipzig, 1978, in *L'Antiquité Classique* 49, 1980, p. 456.

56   Review of M. Mayrhofer, *Ausgewählte kleine Schriften*, Wiesbaden, 1979, in *Onoma* 24, 1980, pp. 261-262.

57   Review of G. Neumann, *Neufunde lykischer Inschriften seit 1902*, Wien, 1979, in *Onoma* 24, 1980, pp. 262-264.

1981

58   "L'Iran réformé ou les malheurs du guerrier," in *Georges Dumézil*, Cahiers pour un temps, Paris, 1981, pp. 157-172.

1983

59   "Die Religion der Achämeniden," *AoF* 10, 1983, pp. 107-123.

60   "État présent des études avestiques," *Orientalia Romana* 5, 1983, pp. 19-30.

61   "Yasna 46, 1 et un aspect de l'idéologie politique iranienne," *Studia Iranica* 12, 1983, pp. 143-150.

62   "Remarques sur la tradition manuscrite du Nīrangistān avestique," *MSS* 42, 1983, pp. 75-95.

1984

63   "Qui était Zarathustra?" in *Les civilisations orientales: figures de Proue*, Université de Liège, Faculté de philosophie et lettres, Conférences, G7, Liège, 1984.

64   "Yima, magicien entre les dieux et les hommes," in *Orientalia J. Duchesne-Guillemin Oblata*, Acta Iranica 23, Leiden, 1984, pp. 267-281.

65   *Le verbe avestique*, Wiesbaden, 1984.

66   "Ahura Mazdā ou Mazdā Ahura?," *MSS* 43, 1984, pp. 133-136.

1985

67   "Mazdak et les soulèvements populaires mazdakites," *Bulletin de la Section belge de l'International Association for the History of Religions*, Liège, 1985, pp. 9-16 (translation of W. Sundermann, "Mazdak und die Mazdakitischen Volksaufstände," *Das Altertum* 23, 1977, pp. 245-249).

68   "Le système modal du vieux-perse," *MSS* 45 (Festgabe für Karl Hoffmann), 1985, pp. 105-125.

69   "Le témoignage du vieil-avestique sur la syntaxe du verbe indo-européen," presentation at the Journée du Cercle des Linguistes belges, Liège, 1985 (private printing).

1986

70   "Artazostre," in *Encyclopaedia Iranica* II/6, London and New York, 1986, p. 660.

71   "La racine sanscrite KAMP à la lumière des faits iraniens," in W. Morgenroth, ed., *Sanskrit and World Culture: Proceedings of the Fourth World Sanskrit Conference of the International Association of Sanskrit Studies, Weimar, May 23-30*, Schriften zur Geschichte und Kultur des alten Orients 18, Berlin, 1986, pp. 344-347.

72   "Comment faut-il éditer les formes vieil-avestiques de *paoiriia-*?," in R. Schmitt and P. O. Skjærvø, eds., *Studia Grammatica Iranica. Festschrift für Helmut Humbach*, Munich, 1986, pp. 217-226.

1987

73   "Sur une hétéroclisie verbale avestique," *IIJ* 30, 1987, pp. 9-12.

74   "Quatre siècles obscurs," in Societas Iranologica Europaea, *Transition Periods in Iranian History, Actes du symposium de Fribourg-en-Brisgau (22-24 mai 1985)*, Studia Iranica, cahier 5, Paris, 1987, pp. 135-139.

75   "Characters of Ancient Mazdaism," *History and Anthropology* 3, 1987, pp. 239-262.

76   "DB V: un témoignage sur l'évolution de l'idéologie achéménide," in G. Gnoli and L. Lanciotti, eds., *Orientalia Iosephi Tucci Memoriae Dicata* II, Rome, 1987, pp. 677-682.

77   "Le sandhi des finales devant °*cā* en vieil-avestique," *MSS* 48, 1987, pp. 167-174.

1988

78   "Avesta," in *Encyclopaedia Iranica* III/1, London, 1988, pp. 35-44.

79   With E. Pirart: *Les textes vieil-avestiques*, 3 vols., Wiesbaden, 1988, 1990, 1991.

80   "Yima et la mort," in M. A. Jazayery and W. Winter, eds., *Languages and Cultures. Studies in Honor of Edgar C. Polomé*, Berlin, New York, Amsterdam, 1988, pp. 329-34.

81   "Une variation du timbre de l'anaptyxe en vieil-avestique," *A Green Leaf. Papers in Honour of Jes P. Asmussen*, Acta Iranica 28, Leiden 1988, pp. 13-15.

82   Review of *Papers in Honour of Professor Mary Boyce*, Acta Iranica 24-25, Leiden, 1985, in *Wiener Zeitschrift für die Kunde des Morgenlandes* 75, 1988, pp. 299-301.

83   "Vohu Manah ou Manah Vohu?" *MSS* 49, 1988, pp. 61-62.

1989

84   "Les Fravaši," in J. Ries, ed., *Anges et démons*, Louvain-la-Neuve, 1989, pp. 99-114.

85   "Avestique," in R. Schmitt, ed., *Compendium Linguarum Iranicarum*, Wiesbaden, 1989, pp. 32-55.

86   "Ahura Mazdā n'est pas un dieu créateur," in Ch.-H. de Fouchécour and Ph. Gignoux, eds., *Études irano-aryennes offertes à Gilbert Lazard*, Studia Iranica, cahier 7, Paris, 1989, pp. 217-28.

87   "Le sens de vieil-avestique *hātạm*," *MSS* 50, 1989, pp. 51-64.

88   "Huttes cosmiques en Iran," *MSS* 50, 1989, pp. 65-78.

1990

89   *La cosmogonie mazdénne ancienne: huttes cosmiques en Iran*, Faculté ouverte (G 28), Liège, 1990.

90   "Méthodes pour une nouvelle interprétation des Gāθā: la question du *śleṣa*," in G. Gnoli and A. Panaino, eds., *Proceedings of the The first European Conference of Iranian Studies*, pt. 1, Rome, 1990, pp. 207-216.

91   "Un avis sur vieil-avestique *mainiiu-*," *MSS* 51, 1990, pp. 97-123.

1991

92   "Questions préalables," in J. Kellens, ed., *La religion iranienne à l'époque achéménide. Actes du Colloque de Liège 11 décembre 1987*, Iranica Antiqua, Suppl. 5, Gent, 1991, pp. 81-86.

93   "Remarques sur l'opposition de nombre en vieil-avestique," in R. E. Emmerick and D. Weber, eds., *Corolla Iranica, papers in honour of*

Prof. D. N. MacKenzie on the occasion of his 65th birthday on April 8th, 1991, Frankfurt, 1991, pp. 101-108.

94   *Zoroastre et l'Avesta ancien. Quatre leçons au Collège de France*, Travaux de l'Institut d'Études Iraniennes de l'Université de la Sorbonne Nouvelle 14, Paris, 1991.

95   "Forschungsbericht: l'avestique de 1972 à 1990," *Kratylos* 36, 1991, pp. 1-31.

96   "Cistā/Cisti," in *Encyclopaedia Iranica* V/6, Costa Mesa, 1991, pp. 601-602.

1992

97   *Titres et travaux de Jean Kellens*, Liège, 1992 (private print).

1993

98   *Qui était Zarathustra?*, Faculté ouverte (G 7, version remaniée), Liège, 1993.

99   *La mort indo-iranienne*, Faculté ouverte (G 34), Liège, 1993.

100   With C. Herrenschmidt: "*Daiva*," in *Encyclopaedia Iranica* VI/6, Costa Mesa, 1993, pp. 599-602.

101   "*Dāmi*," in *Encyclopaedia Iranica* VI/6, Costa Mesa, 1993, pp. 638-639.

1994

102   "Avesta," in B. Didier, ed., *Dictionnaire universel des littératures*, Paris, 1994, pp. 275-276.

103   "Zarathustra," in B. Didier, ed., *Dictionnaire universel des littératures*, Paris, 1994, p. 4222.

104   "L'eschatologie mazdéenne ancienne," in S. Shaked and A. Netzer, eds., *Irano-Judaica* III, Jerusalem, 1994, pp. 49-53.

105   "La fonction aurorale de Miθra et la daēnā," in J.R. Hinnells, ed., *Studies in Mithraism*, Rome, 1994, pp. 165-171.

106   "Le rituel spéculatif du mazdéisme ancien," in Kellens and C. Herrenschmidt, "La question du rituel dans le mazdéisme ancien et

achéménide," *Archives de Sciences sociales des Religions* 85, 1994, pp. 45-67 (47-56).

107   *Leçon inaugurale de la chaire de langues et religions indo-iraniennes du Collège de France*, Paris, 1994.

108   *Le panthéon de l'Avesta ancien*, Wiesbaden, 1994.

109   "Dēn Yašt," in *Encyclopaedia Iranica* VI/3, Costa Mesa, 1994, pp. 281-282.

1995

110   "Retour à l'infinitif avestique," *MSS*, 1994 [1995], 45-59.

111   "Formules d'exécration et mimes de combat dans le rituel mazdéen ancien," *Le Temple lieu de conflit*, CEPOA 7, Genève, 1995, pp. 89-94.

112   "Qui est Gōuš Tašan?" in B.G. Fragner et al., eds., *Proceedings of the Second European Conference of Iranian Studies*, Rome, 1995, pp. 347-57.

113   *Liste du verbe avestique* (avec un appendice sur l'orthographe des racines avestiques par Eric Pirart), Wiesbaden, 1995.

114   *Trois discours de circonstance*, Discours prononcés l'occasion de l'élection de Jean Kellens au Collège de France, Liège, 1995 (private print).

115   "Résumé des cours et travaux de la chaire de langues et religions indo-iraniennes," *Annuaire du Collège de France 1993-1994*, Paris, 1995, pp. 721-722.

116   "Y a-t-il une âme osseuse?" in R. Gyselen, ed., *Au carrefour des religions. Hommages à Philippe Gignoux*, Res Orientales 7, Paris, 1995, pp. 157-60.

117   "Arta," in K. van der Toorn et al., eds., *Dictionary of Deities and Demons in the Bible*, Leiden, 1995, pp. 165-167.

118   "Baga," in K. van der Toorn et al., eds., *Dictionary of Deities and Demons in the Bible*, Leiden, 1995, pp. 304-305.

119   "Haoma," in K. van der Toorn et al., eds., *Dictionary of Deities and Demons in the Bible*, Leiden, 1995, pp. 729-731.

120   "L'âme entre le cadavre et le paradis," *JA* 283, 1995, pp. 19-56.

121   "Interrogation," *JA* 283, 1995, pp. 271-274.

1996

122 "*Druj-*," in *Encyclopaedia Iranica* VII/6, Costa Mesa, 1996, pp. 562-563.

123 "*Drvāspā-*," in *Encyclopaedia Iranica* VII/6, Costa Mesa, 1996, p. 565.

124 "*Dūraoša-*," in *Encyclopaedia Iranica* VII/6, Costa Mesa, 1996, pp. 595-596.

125 "Résumé des cours et travaux de la chaire de langues et religions indo-iraniennes," *Annuaire du Collège de France 1994-1995*, 1996, pp. 697-705.

126 "Commentaire sur les premiers chapitres du Yasna," *JA* 284, 1996, pp. 37-108.

127 "The Written Period of Transmission of the Avesta," *The Journal of the Research and Historical Preservation Committee* 2, 1996, pp. 121-125.

128 "Comment connaissons-nous l'Avesta, le livre sacré des mazdéens?" *Bulletin de la Classe des Lettres de l'Académie royale de Belgique*, 1996 (7-12), pp. 497-508.

1997

129 "Résumé des cours et travaux de la chaire de langues et religions indo-iraniennes," *Annuaire du Collège de France 1995-1996*, 1997, pp. 775-776.

130 "Les fonctions du génitif en vieil-avestique," in E. Pirart, ed., *Syntaxe des langues indo-iraniennes anciennes*, *Colloque international de Sitges 4-5 mai 1993*, Aula Orientalis Supplementa, Barcelona 1997, pp. 81-90.

131 "Le mazdéisme," in F. Lenoir et Y. Tardan-Masquelier, eds., *Encyclopédie des religions* I: *Histoire*, Paris, 1997, pp. 105-117.

132 "L'accusatif pluriel des thèmes en -*a*- en avestique," in A. Lubotsky, ed., *Sound Law and Analogy. Papers in Honor of Robert S. P. Beekes*, Amsterdam, 1997, pp. 131-132.

133 With Eric Pirart: "La strophe des jumeaux: stagnation, extravagance et autres méthodes d'approche," *JA* 285, 1997, pp. 31-72.

134   "Les achéménides dans le contexte indo-iranien," *Topoì Supplément* I, Lyon, 1997, pp. 287-297.

1998

135   "Résumé des cours et travaux de la chaire de langues et religions indo-iraniennes," *Annuaire du Collège de France 1996-1997*, 1998, pp. 747-748.

136   "Comment connaissons-nous l'Avesta, le livre sacré des mazdéens (II)," *Bulletin de la Classe des Lettres de l'Académie royale de Belgique*, 1998 (1-6), pp. 54-74.

137   "Considérations sur l'histoire de l'Avesta," *JA* 286, 1998, pp. 451-519.

138   "De la naissance des montagnes à la fin du temps: le Yašt 19. Résumé des cours et travaux de la chaire de langues et religions indo-iraniennes," *Annuaire du Collège de France 1997-1998*, 1998, pp. 737-765.

1999

139   "Hypallages de la diction," *Studia Iranica* 28, 1999, pp. 293-295.